JEWELRY MAKING BY
THE LOST WAX PROCESS

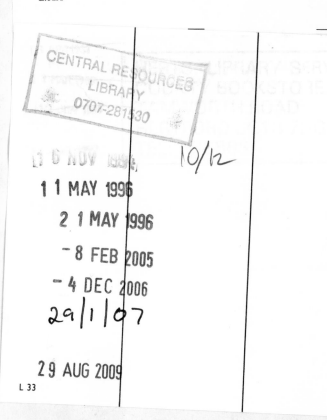

JEWELRY MAKING BY THE LOST WAX PROCESS

by

GRETA PACK

Drawings by

LAURINE MUETHEL HOUGHTON

Photographs by

ELMER L. ASTLEFORD

ROBERT SINGHAUS

D. VAN NOSTRAND COMPANY, INC.

PRINCETON, NEW JERSEY

Toronto   London   Melbourne

56/0868

VAN NOSTRAND REGIONAL OFFICES:
New York, Chicago, San Francisco

D. VAN NOSTRAND COMPANY, LTD., London

D. VAN NOSTRAND COMPANY (Canada), LTD., Toronto

D. VAN NOSTRAND AUSTRALIA PTY. LTD., Melbourne

B68-17453.

Library of Congress Catalog Card No. 68–19368

PRINTED IN THE UNITED STATES OF AMERICA

To

MARY L. DAVIS

PREFACE

Recently, one of the most ancient methods of metal casting, the *cire-perdue* or "Lost Wax Process," has been revived. This is a process by which jewelry is cast in a mold formed from a wax pattern that has been encased in a plaster-like material (investment) which withstands intense heat without cracking. The mold thus formed is placed in a furnace and the heat is brought up slowly. The invested pattern melts, the wax runs out of the opening (sprue hole) left in the casing, and the wax is "lost." Hence the name "Lost Wax Process" given this method of casting. Into the mold formed by the melting of the wax, molten metal (gold, silver, or other casting metal) is thrown by centrifugal force. The encased casting is submerged in water; the investment disintegrates and releases the metal casting, which then requires very little finishing.

Originally this process was done with primitive tools and materials found in the countryside. Wax of the wild bee and copal from the tropical trees were mixed and rolled into sheets, then formed into the pattern to be cast. Clay and charcoal ground and mixed together were used to encase the pattern. When thoroughly dry the pattern was melted out through an opening, leaving the mold into which the molten metal was poured.

Much of the beautiful pre-Hispanic gold work was made

using this process, which was brought up the Pacific coast from Peru, Costa Rica, and Panama, and may have originated in the Americas. In Oaxaca, Mexico, the gold centers of the Mixtecs and Zapotecs, the *cire-perdue* process was used to make some of the finest gold jewelry. The gold treasure discovered in recent years in the burial vault of Monte Alban Tomb #7 was the work of Mixtec goldsmiths. Many of the original pieces are in the Oaxaca Museum not far from where they were found and contemporary Oaxaca goldsmiths are producing beautiful reproductions using the "Lost Wax Process."

There are several other methods used in casting jewelry by pressing a pattern which can be carved or modeled easily from material such as wood or soft metal. The pattern is placed between two iron frames packed with casting sand and pressed together. When the frames are separated and the pattern removed a mold is left; a channel is cut in the sand from the mold to the frames; the frames are then clamped together and the molten metal is poured in.

This same method is followed by pressing the pattern into the smooth, porous surface of cuttlebone. Or the mold can be carved in a light volcanic stone, a form of tuff, used by many Indians of the southwest. Using any of these three methods, when the casting is released from the mold it is rough and the edges have to be filed and the surface made smooth with abrasives.

The "Lost Wax Process" is used now almost universally by manufacturing jewelers and individual craftsmen. New tools and materials are now available and the craftsman has more freedom in designing (undercuts in the pattern do not break the mold; also finer detail is possible).

While reproductions of nature can be cast, it is of course much more satisfactory in designing jewelry to use shapes, rhythms, and patterns found in nature, transposing and changing the proportions and combinations.

CONTENTS

I. Jewelry Making by the Lost Wax Process

Tools and Working Materials
Waxes
Preparation for Casting
Casting

JEWELRY MAKING BY THE
LOST WAX PROCESS

The method of jewelry casting described in this book is the more recent method of casting jewelry, by means of a casting machine operated by centrifugal force, in a mold made of dental investment.

Following the description of the casting process are fourteen projects illustrating wax patterns to be cast using different waxes and methods. Most of these pattern designs were derived from forms found in nature. Using these as examples, you will be able to design your own patterns. When the pattern has been finished, the procedure to be followed is the same for all projects—preparation of the metal, mounting and investing the pattern, casting and finishing—followed by whatever final ornamentation the design calls for. The metal used for casting throughout this book is sterling silver, though gold and other casting metals may be used following the same procedure. At the back of the book are reviewed procedures for annealing, pickling, soldering, etc., processes which occur repeatedly in the course of construction of a piece of jewelry. Additional projects for casting jewelry by the Lost Wax Process can be found in *Jewelry and Enameling*, accessory items (chains, twisted and coiled wire, etc.) in *Chains and Beads*, both by this author.*

TOOLS AND WORKING MATERIALS

Tracing paper
Carbon paper
Lubricant—microfilm
Glass slab
Wax
Tripod
Alcohol
Alcohol lamp
Mesh screen
Melting pan—small
Scratch awl
Dapping die block
Dapping dies
Knife
Gravers
Gauge (Brown and Sharpe)
Spatulas (spoon, knife)
Graduated cylinder
Sprue pin
Sprue former
Vacufilm (or Debubblizer)
Camel's hair brush
Asbestos strip
Asbestos crucible liners

Bench pin
Jeweler's saw frame
Jeweler's saw blades, No. 1, No. 2
Hacksaw
Jeweler's pliers, flat and round nose
Bench vise
Hand drill
Twist drills
Dividers
Jeweler's shears
Tweezers
Charcoal block
Solder
Solder flux
Binding wire
Files, 6-inch flat and half-round
Needle files
Emery cloth
Scotch stone
Soda Bicarbonate solution
Sandpaper

* Greta Pack, *Jewelry and Enameling* (3rd ed.; Princeton, N.J.: D. Van Nostrand, Publishing Company, Inc., 1961); *Chains and Beads* (Princeton, N.J.: D. Van Nostrand Company, Inc., 1952).

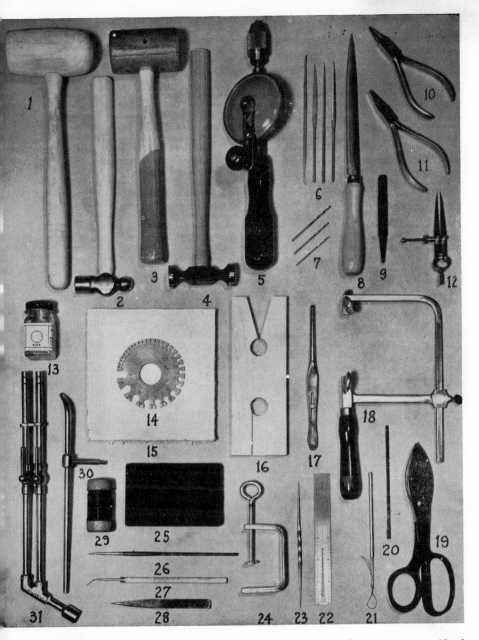

Fig. 1. Wood mallet; 2. Ballpeen hammer; 3. Rawhide mallet; 4. Planishing Hammer; 5. Hand drill; 6. Needle files; 7. Twist drills; 8. Half round file; 9. Center punch; 10. Round nose pliers; 11. Flat nose pliers; 12. Dividers; 13. Soldering Flux; 14. B&S Wire gauge; 15. Asbestos block; 16. Bench pin; 17. Soldering tweezers; 18. Jeweler's saw frame; 19. Jeweler's shears; 20. Jeweler's saw blades; 21. Dentimetre; 22. Steel rule; 23. Scratch awl; 24. Bench pin; 25. Charcoal block; 26. Soldering brush; 27. Spatula; 28. Tweezers; 29. Binding wire; 30. Mouth blow torch; 31. Gas & air blow torch.

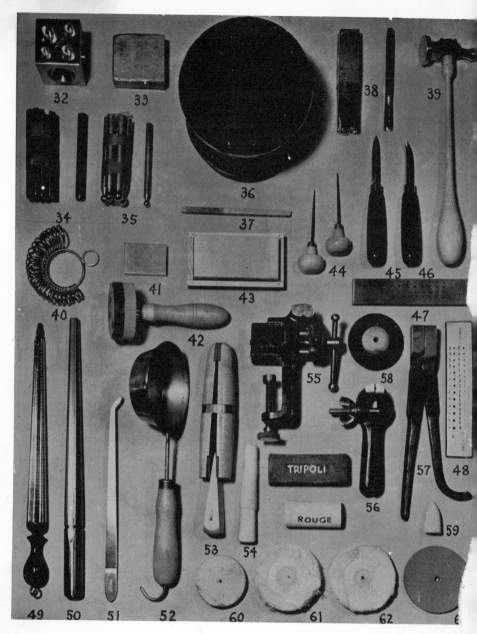

Fig. 2. 32. Dapping die; 33. Lead dapping block; 34. Dapping die cutters; 35. Dapping punches; 36. Pitch bowl; 37. Scotch stone; 38. Chasing, repousse, tools; 39. Chasing hammer 40. Ring sizes; 41. Steel surface plate; 42. Shellac stick; 43. Oil stone; 44. Gravers; 45. Scrape 46. Burnisher; 47. Square hole draw plate; 48. Round hole draw plate; 49. Ring gauge; 50 Ring mandrel; 51. Copper tongs; 52. Pickle pan; 53. Ring clamps; 54. Felt ring buff; 55. Table vise; 56. Hand vise; 57. Draw tongs; 58. Bristle buffing wheel; 59. Felt cone; 60. Felt buff wheel; 61. Muslin buffing wheel; 62. Chamois buffing wheel; 63. Emery grinding wheel.

Flasks—stainless steel cylinders in several sizes
Dental investment
Rubber mixing bowl
Mixing spatula
Furnace—controlled heat
Metal tray, steel
Trivet, metal or stoneware
Iron tongs
Clay crucible
Reducing flux
Blowtorch
Centrifico Casting Machine*
Pickle—sulfuric acid solution
　　—nitric acid solution
　　—Sparex solution No. 2
Pickle pan, copper
Tweezers, copper

Polishing motor, flexible shaft
Tripoli, felt buff, bristle buff
Rouge stick, cloth buff, chamois buff
Soda, ammonia, and water solution
Potassium sulfide solution
Dentimeter
Ring mandrel—graduated
Ring clamp
Stone-setting tool
Stone lifter
Riveting hammer—steel
Burnisher
Shellac stick
Epoxy cement
Regular Permlastic Impression material

WAXES

Many new wax products have been developed for the jewelry craftsman designing and making wax patterns for centrifugal-force casting, using the Lost Wax Process. The wax is available in many forms—in sheets and ready-made wire of various gauges, in stick form, blocks, and cakes—and varies in hardness. There are several different methods used in making wax patterns, depending upon the type of wax selected. Some of the patterns are made with only one type of wax; others combine

---

* The standard Kerr Centrifico Casting Machine comes with stainless steel flasks, in several sizes, and clay crucibles. A large bronze casting arm can be mounted on the same base, replacing the standard arm, to take larger flasks and greater crucible capacity.

several waxes. Choice of wax often depends upon the design and construction of the article.

The colors of waxes vary and are used as codes by the manufacturers.

Blue Carving	Block form, firm and brittle; carving, hot tools and flaming.
Karvex	Block form, three grades of hardness:
	1. Green—very hard: machine tools, filing, carving, etc.
	2. Purple—hard: may be carved, filed, and sanded; hot tools and flaming, etc.
	3. Blue—not as hard as Karvex No. 2: for hand-carving and hot-tool forming.
Green Wax Sheets	Soft, requires no heat. 3½ inches square.
Pink Wax Sheets	Transparent, less flexible than the green. 3½ inches square.
	(Both green and pink wax sheets are thin, smooth, and flexible; 22-, 24-, and 26-gauge.)
Wire shapes (ready-made)	Four-inch lengths in several gauges. Round, half-round, pear-shaped. Pliable, may be twisted or bent (see p. 79). May be welded together to add length to wire. Often whole patterns are made entirely of wire. May be used for sprues in mounting wax patterns for casting.

Sculpture Wax

Hand forming; never hardens, but holds its form for sculpturing; may be rolled and bent.

Soluble Wax

Water soluble, for making expendable mandrels or cores; may be machined, carved, and sawed.

Wax Sheets (mixed waxes)

Carving wax melted with blending wax or pink wax sheet poured on a lubricated glass slab to form wax sheet. When cool, add more wax. Repeat to the gauge desired. May be bent or carved. The amount of each wax used depends upon the flexibility desired.

WORKING WAXES

Tac Wax

Used to weld two or more pieces together; fast setting.

Utility Wax

Plastic at room temperature; used in the sprue former to hold the sprue pin and to hold the flask to the sprue former.

Sticky Wax

Used like cement for holding wax parts together. Comes in stick form.

CASTING

Once the pattern has been shaped, the mold is formed by encasing the pattern in dental investment. Casting, or dental, investment comes in powder form. It is mixed with water to a creamy consistency and is poured over the pattern which has been set in a flask. The mold thus formed, when hard, is smooth and can be heated without cracking. The procedure described here for preparing the casting, forming the mold, and casting is the same for all of the projects which follow.

PREPARATION FOR CASTING

PREPARING THE SILVER

To measure the amount of silver required, fill a graduate cylinder partly full of water (Fig. 3). Fasten a fine wire on the wax pattern and lower it into the cylinder (Fig. 4). Note the amount of water displaced by the pattern. Remove the pattern from the cylinder; note that the water recedes to the original mark on the graduated scale. Drop enough metal into the cylinder to bring the water up to the line registered when the pattern was in the cylinder. Add a little more silver to raise the water about 2 cc. or ml. to allow for the wax to be used for the sprue pin and wax ball. Pickle the metal (p. 87).

MOUNTING THE PATTERN

Warm one end of the metal sprue pin and insert it ⅛ inch into the thickest part of the pattern. Seal with wax. Rings are sprued to the back of the shank opposite the top (Fig. 5). Tilt the pattern slightly, if there is a flat surface in the interior, parallel to the base of the sprue former.

Add wax sprues if any part of the pattern is below the point where the pattern is sealed to the pin. Add extra sprues if the circumference of the pattern is some distance from the main sprue. Seal a ¼-inch wax ball on the sprue pin ⅟₁₆ of an inch from the pattern. Double the thickness of the pin between the pattern and the ball (Fig. 5). Hold the pin in the sprue former with utility wax.

Fig. 3. Graduate cylin-
der containing water
for measuring.

Fig. 4. Measuring the
volume of the wax
pattern.

Wash the wax surface with water using a soft brush or absorbent cotton. Paint the pattern with lubricant and let dry before investing the pattern.

> NOTE: Lubricant—Vacufilm or Debubblizer—is painted on a wax pattern before investing to reduce the surface tension and cause the investment to flow smoothly. Microfilm, also a lubricant, is painted on a glass surface before pouring melted wax on it to form a sheet, or on a stone when shaping the wax to form a setting.

INVESTING THE PATTERN

Line the flask with damp asbestos sheet ¼ inch from each edge and with a ½-inch overlap.

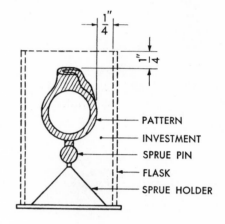

Fig. 5. The size of the flask depends upon the size of the wax pattern, when on the sprue pin and sprue former. The top of the pattern should not be more than one-half inch from the top rim of the flask or closer than one-quarter inch from the top and sides.

PATTERN
INVESTMENT
SPRUE PIN
FLASK
SPRUE HOLDER

Measure out the amount of investment plus a little more than the flask will hold. Use a rubber bowl for mixing. Add water (70–72 degrees F.) to the investment, a little at a time. Mix with a spatula to a thick creamy consistency; vibrate the bowl for several seconds to release the air bubbles.

Cover the pattern and ball with mixed investment about ⅛ inch thick. Vibrate. Do not let the investment on the pattern dry completely before filling the flask. Center the mounted pattern in the flask. Seal the flask to the rim of the sprue former with utility wax. Fill the flask with investment. Vibrate the flask.

> NOTE: When the sprue former is too small for the rim of the flask, seal the sprue former to a glass surface with utility wax before the pattern is invested in the flask.

Another way to invest the pattern is to seal the flask to a glass surface and insert the mounted pattern coated with investment into the flask filled with investment, letting the rim of the sprue former rest on the rim of the flask.

It takes about one hour after the pattern has been encased for the investment to set and it is ready for the burnout. When the investment has set, remove the sprue former and sprue pin; smooth the top and clean the sides of the flask of investment.

BALANCING THE MACHINE

Before the flask is heated, place the cradle to fit the flask on the arm of the machine and place the invested flask in the cradle, on the same end of the arm as the saddle holding the crucible containing the metal to be cast. The other end of the arm of the counterweight is placed on the horizontal rod. Balance the machine; tighten the nut to hold the arm firmly.

FORMING THE MOLD

Heat the flask to eliminate the wax to form the mold. The time varies with the size of the flask. A 3 × 3½ inch flask takes about eight hours for the burnout.

Preheat the furnace to 200 degrees F. Put a metal or porcelain trivet on a steel tray. Put the invested flask on the trivet, sprue hole down, and place in the furnace. Hold the 200-degree temperature for two hours. At the end of this period, turn the flask so that the sprue hole is up. Advance the heat 200 degrees each hour; the seventh hour when 1200 degrees has been reached, turn the sprue hole down and hold for one hour.

Lower the temperature to 650 degrees for the silver casting and allow the furnace to cool down.

PREPARING THE CRUCIBLE

Place a damp asbestos pad in the crucible. Sprinkle reducing flux on the pad. Heat to fuse the flux and to heat the crucible, which must be hot when the flask reaches the casting temperature and is placed in the cradle on the machine. Place the silver to be cast in the crucible; sprinkle with flux. (All the silver may be melted at once or added little by little as the melting takes place.)

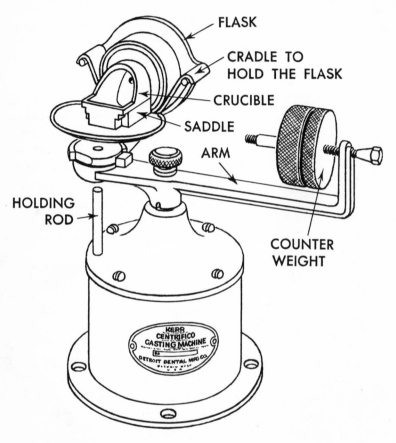

Fig. 6. CENTRIFICO CASTING MACHINE (Courtesy of Kerr Manufacturing Company). The casting machine must be mounted and held firmly to a level bench. There is a heavy spring in the base; the arms of the machine which carry the flask crucible and counterweight rotate horizontally. A shield should be made and held to the bench to prevent molten metal from being thrown into the surrounding area when the spring is released and the molten metal is being forced into the mold.

Remove the flask from the furnace. Place in the cradle on the arm of the carrier with the sprue hole facing the crucible (Fig. 6). The lip of the crucible must fit into the sprue opening. Push the saddle close to the rim of the flask. *Casting should be done as soon as possible after the hot flask has been removed from the furnace, as the investment cools very quickly.*

CASTING

Turn the arm of the carrier two times to wind the spring; push up the stop rod to lock the carrier.

Heat the metal with the blowtorch. Hold the blowtorch so the flame is perpendicular to the metal; in this position the torch will not have to be changed when the metal melts into the bottom of the crucible. Direct on the metal the part of the flame which lies just above the point of the cone—the hottest part of the flame. A hot flame is necessary because if the metal is heated too slowly it absorbs too much gas, which will leave pit marks in the casting. Overheating of the metal during the melting process should be avoided for the same reason. A steady heat is required until the metal has become fluid. Lift the flame a little.

Sprinkle prepared reducing flux on the metal to keep it from oxidizing during the melting process. Borax powder can also be used but it does not have the reducing quality of prepared reducing flux. When the metal is in a fluid state, but not boiling or spinning, flux the metal and release the stop rod. The arm spins and throws the molten metal from the crucible into the mold. Let the machine stop its spin.

> NOTE: Occasionally a casting is incomplete. This may be because the melted silver was not hot enough to flow into the mold or because the silver was not thrown into the mold under sufficient pressure.

COOLING AND REMOVING THE CASTING

Remove the flask from the casting machine with tongs. Set aside to cool for about five minutes. Pour a small amount of water into a deep pan. Hold the flask so that the investment touches the water for a moment. Remove from the water. Repeat several times. Immerse in water. The investment will disintegrate. Remove the investment from the casting with a stiff brush.

FINISHING

Place the casting on a charcoal block. Heat to a dull red glow. Immerse in pickle (p. 87). Saw off the cast sprues; file the casting to remove any roughness. Sharpen or carve any lines necessary with the gravers. Polish the surface (p. 99).

II.   PROJECTS

RING WITH CORAL STONE AND CARVED DESIGN

PREPARATION OF THE WAX PATTERN

Draw the design; transfer the outline of the shank to heavy paper and cut a paper pattern; measure the ring size.

Spread a thin film of microfilm on a glass slab. Melt carving wax with blending wax. Pour melted wax on the lubricated glass slab. Let the wax cool. Pour more melted wax over it. Repeat to form a sheet ⅛ inch thick. Lay the paper pattern on the wax sheet. Draw around the pattern and cut the pattern from the wax sheet. Carve and model the design with graver (p. 89) and warm spatula. Remove excess wax from the underside, to make the casting lighter in weight.

Lubricate the ring mandrel. Warm the pattern and shape around the mandrel to form the shank one size smaller than the measured ring size, to allow for filing, finishing, and buffing the casting. Seal the joint. Lubricate the stone. Warm the wax for the stone setting with a spatula. Press the stone into the wax. Remove the stone. Refine the carving. Smooth the surface. Wash the pattern under running water, brushing with a soft brush or absorbent cotton.

CASTING

Measure the amount of silver needed for casting the pattern (p. 9). Invest the pattern (p. 10); heat and cast the invested pattern (p. 13).

FINISHING

Saw off sprue pins (p. 89); anneal (p. 85), pickle (p. 87), buff (p. 99), texture with a graver (p. 89). Color with potassium sulfide solution (p. 97). Polish (p. 99). Place stone on shank (p. 76). Hold in place with epoxy cement. Let dry. Tap silver over stone (Fig. 8) and burnish.

PROJECT 1

RING WITH CORAL STONE AND CARVED DESIGN

PATTERN OF WAX

Draw the design. Measure the ring size. Cut a paper pattern.

WAX PATTERN

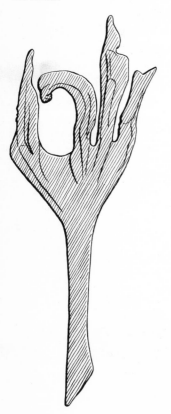

Lubricate a glass slab. Melt carving wax with blending wax. Pour on the slab to form a sheet. Let cool. Repeat to ⅛ inch thickness.

Cut the pattern from the wax. Carve and model the design. Remove excess wax from the underside.

Lubricate a ring mandrel. Warm the wax pattern. Shape around the mandrel to form the shank— one size smaller than the measured size. Seal the joint. Refine the carving. Smooth the surface.

CASTING

Measure the amount of silver required. Seal the pattern to the sprue pin. Seal a ¼-inch ball $\frac{1}{16}$ inch from the pattern. Double the thickness of the pin between the pattern and ball. Seal the sprue pin to the sprue former. Wash in water—use a soft brush or cotton baton.

Paint with vacufilm. Let dry. Line the flask with damp asbestos sheet. Cover the pattern and ball with mixed investment. Seal the flask to the sprue former. Fill the flask with mixed investment. Remove the sprue former and sprue pin when the investment has set. Heat the flask in the furnace. Prepare the crucible. Cast the pattern.

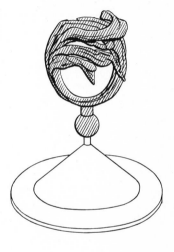

CASTING

FINISHING

Saw off cast sprue pin. Anneal the casting. Clean in pickle. Texture. Color and polish. Hold the stone in place with epoxy cement. Let dry. Tap the silver over the stone.

PROJECT 2

RING WITH CORAL STONES, BEADS, AND CARVED DESIGN

Preparation of the Wax Pattern

Draw the design; trace the design on thin paper; measure the ring size.

Spread a thin film of microfilm on a glass slab. Melt carving wax with blending wax. Pour melted wax on the lubricated glass slab. Let cool. Pour more melted wax over it. Repeat to form a sheet ⅛ inch thick. Lay the tracing on the wax sheet. Prick the design into the wax with the point of a needle. Remove the tracing. Rub white powder over the wax surface. Dust the sheet; the powder will remain in the holes to outline the design. Join the holes with a scratched line and cut along the outline to release the design from the wax sheet. Carve and model the design.

Lubricate the ring mandrel. Warm the pattern and shape around the mandrel to form the shank one size smaller than the measured ring size, to allow for filing, finishing, and buffing of the casting. Seal the joint.

Soften the wax for the stone and bead placement with a spoon spatula. Lubricate the stones and beads with microfilm and press them into the warm wax. Scrape the wax around the stones to a lighter gauge. Remove the stones. Cut openings under the stones and beads for bearings. Refine the carving. Smooth the surface. Wash the pattern under running water, brushing with a soft brush or absorbent cotton.

Casting

Measure the amount of silver needed for casting the pattern (p. 9). Invest the pattern (p. 10); heat and cast the invested pattern (p. 13).

FINISHING

Saw off the sprue pins (p. 89); anneal (p. 85), pickle (p. 87), and buff (p. 99). Texture (p. 89); color with potassium sulfide solution (p. 97); polish (p. 99). Hold beads in place with epoxy cement; bend the silver over the edge of the stones and burnish.

Ring with coral stones and carved design (see Project 1), after seaweed motif.

RING DESIGN

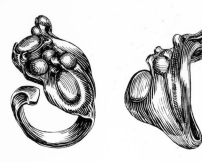

RING WITH CORAL STONES, BEADS, AND CARVED DESIGN

Pattern of Wax

Draw the design. Measure the ring size. Make a tracing. Lubricate a glass slab. Melt carving wax with blending wax. Pour on the glass slab. Let cool. Repeat to ⅛ inch in thickness. Transfer the design to the wax sheet. Cut the wax pattern. Carve and model the design. Lubricate the stones and beads. Press into the warm wax in the position shown. Make openings under the stones and beads (leaving bearings). Remove excess wax from underside.

WAX PATTERN

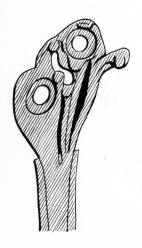

Lubricate the ring mandrel. Warm the pattern. Shape around the mandrel (one size smaller than measured). Seal the joint. Refine the carving. Smooth the surface.

CASTING

Measure the amount of silver required. Mount the pattern on a sprue pin. Seal a $\frac{1}{4}$-inch wax ball $\frac{1}{16}$ inch from the pattern. Double the thickness of the pin between pattern and ball. Seal the pin to the sprue former. Wash with water —use a soft brush or absorbent cotton. Paint with vacufilm. Let dry. Cover the pattern with mixed investment. Line the flask with damp asbestos sheet. Seal the flask to the sprue former. Fill the flask with mixed investment before the invested pattern is completely dry. Remove the sprue former and sprue pin when the investment has set. Heat the flask in the furnace. Prepare the crucible. Cast the pattern.

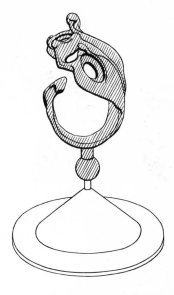

CASTING

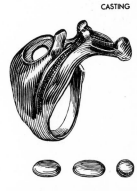

FINISHING

Saw off cast sprue. Anneal the casting. Clean in pickle. Texture. Color and polish. Burnish the silver over the edge of the stones. Hold the beads in place with epoxy cement.

Attractive design ideas can be found in natural forms.

RING WITH OVAL STONE AND
CARVED DESIGN

PREPARATION OF THE WAX PATTERN

Draw the design; make four tracings, two of the shank and two of the carved design; measure the ring size.

Place Green Karvex 1¼-inch rod in the jaws of the table vise. Saw the length (p. 89). Place the tracing of the shank on the Karvex. Prick the design into the wax with the point of a needle. Repeat on the other side. Remove the tracing. Rub white powder over the wax surface. Dust the sheet; the powder will remain in the holes to outline the design. Join the holes with a scratched line.

Make a circle with dividers, one size smaller than the measured ring size to allow for filing, finishing, and buffing of the casting. Rub white powder over the wax surface. Dust off, leaving a white outline of the ring shank. Drill a hole. Saw the center and outline to form the ring shank. Carve, file (p. 89).

Transfer the carved design to the sides, pricking the design out as above. Carve and file the design. Smooth the surface. Wash the pattern in water, brushing with a soft brush or absorbent cotton.

CASTING

Measure the amount of silver needed for the casting (p. 9). Invest the pattern (p. 10); heat and cast the invested pattern (p. 13).

FINISHING

Saw off the sprue pins (p. 89); anneal (p. 85), pickle (p. 87), buff (p. 99), color with potassium sulfide solution (p. 97), and polish (p. 99). Set the stone (p. 76).

RING WITH OVAL STONE AND CARVED DESIGN

WAX PATTERN

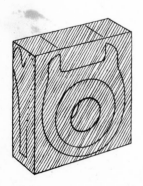

PATTERN OF WAX

Measure the ring size. Make two tracings of each: the ring shank and the design. Draw the design. Saw a length of Green Karvex wax from a 1¼-inch rod. Lay the traced outline of the shank on the wax. Pin prick the outline into the wax. Remove the tracing and rub white powder over the wax surface. Carve a line in the wax to connect the transfer. Rub white powder over the surface.

Make a circle one size smaller than measured. Drill a hole. Saw the outline and center to form the ring shank. File, carve, and finish (machine tools may be used). Transfer (as shown) the carved design from the tracing to the shank. Carve the design, file, and shape. Wash with water—use a soft brush or absorbent cotton.

CASTING

Measure the amount of silver required. Seal the pattern to the sprue pin. Seal a ¼-inch ball to the sprue pin ¹⁄₁₆ inch from the pattern.

Double the thickness between the pattern and the ball. Seal the pin to the sprue former. Paint the pattern with vacufilm. Let dry. Cover the wax surface with mixed investment. Do not allow it to dry completely before filling the flask.

Line the flask with damp asbestos sheet. Seal the flask to the sprue former. Fill the flask with mixed investment; vibrate to release air bubbles. Remove the flask from the sprue former when the investment has set. Cast the pattern.

CASTING

FINISHING

Saw off cast sprue pin. Clean in pickle. Color and polish. Set the stone.

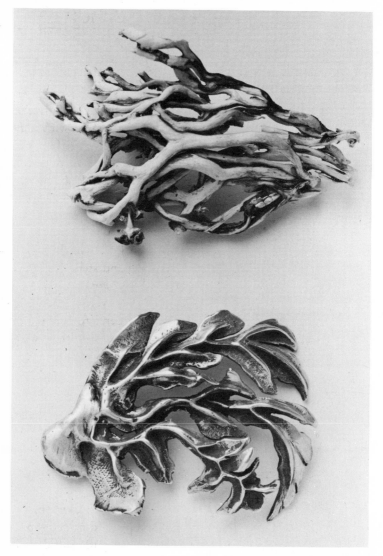

Brooch with carved design (Project 4) and driftwood motif.

BROOCH WITH CARVED DESIGN

Preparation of the Wax Pattern

Draw the design; trace the veins and stems.

Place a chunk of soluble wax in the jaws of the table vise. Saw a flat surface with a hacksaw (p. 89), slightly larger than the design and ¼ inch thick. Smooth the surface with a file and sandpaper. Transfer the tracing to the wax surface with carbon paper. Carve intaglio ⅛ inch in depth with a graver.

Spread a thin film of microfilm on a glass slab. Place the wax on the slab, carved side up. Melt carving wax with blending wax. Pour the melted wax over the carved surface. Let cool. Repeat to a thickness of 12-gauge.

Place the wax in a bowl of cold water to dissolve the soluble wax, leaving a wax sheet with raised veins and stems. Lay the sheet on the glass slab. Cut around the design to release the pattern from the sheet. Carve with a graver. Model and smooth with a warm spatula. Warm and bend to form. Remove excess wax from the back of the pattern with a warm spoon spatula to make the casting lighter in weight.

Casting

Measure the amount of silver needed for casting the pattern (p. 9). Invest the pattern (p. 10); heat and cast the invested pattern (p. 13).

Finishing

Saw off the sprue pins (p. 89); anneal (p. 85), pickle (p. 87), and buff (p. 99). Bind and solder the joint and catch in place (p. 94). Pickle (p. 87), and color with potassium sulfide solution (p. 97), and polish (p. 99). Rivet the pin stem in the joint (p. 94).

BROOCH DESIGN

BROOCH WITH CARVED DESIGN

PATTERN OF WAX

Draw the design. Trace the veins and stems. Saw and smooth soluble wax (a piece slightly larger than the drawing and ¼ inch thick). Transfer the tracing onto the prepared surface with carbon paper. Carve intaglio ⅛ inch in depth.

WAX PATTERN

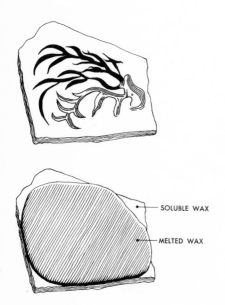

SOLUBLE WAX

MELTED WAX

Lubricate a glass slab. Place the wax on the glass carved side up. Melt carving wax with blending wax. Pour over the wax surface to fill the carving and form a wax sheet. Let the wax cool. Repeat to a thickness of 12 gauge. Place in a bowl of cold water to dissolve the soluble wax, leaving a wax sheet with raised veins and stems. Cut the wax pattern. Carve and model the design. Warm and bend to form. Remove excess wax from the back of the pattern.

Casting

Measure the amount of silver required for the casting. Mount the
pattern on a sprue pin. Seal a $\frac{1}{4}$-
inch ball $\frac{1}{16}$ inch from the pattern. Double the thickness of the
pin between the pattern and ball.
Add extra sprues.

Seal the sprue pin to the sprue
former. Wash in water—use a soft
brush or absorbent cotton. Paint
with vacufilm.

Cover the pattern and wax ball
with investment $\frac{1}{8}$ inch thick. Do
not let it dry before the flask is
filled with investment. Line the
flask with damp asbestos sheet.
Seal the flask to the sprue former.

Fill the flask with mixed investment. Remove the sprue former and
sprue pin when the investment has
set. Pickle the metal to be cast.
Heat the flask in the furnace. Prepare the crucible. Cast the pattern.

CASTING

Finishing

Saw off cast sprues. Anneal the
casting. Clean in pickle. Texture.
Bind and solder the joint and catch
in place. Clean, color, and polish.
Rivet the pin stem in the joint.

Brooch with carved design derived from fungus motif (Project 5).

BROOCH WITH CARVED DESIGN

PREPARATION OF THE WAX PATTERN

Draw the design. Trace the design.

Spread a thin film of microfilm on a glass slab. Melt carving wax with blending wax. Pour melted wax on the lubricated glass slab. Let cool. Pour more melted wax over it. Repeat to form a sheet ⅛ inch thick. Lay the tracing on the wax sheet. Prick the design into the wax with the point of a needle. Rub white powder over the wax surface. Dust the surface; the powder will remain in the holes to outline the design. Follow the transfer with a pointed graver. Dust with white powder, leaving a white outline of the design. Cut along the outline to release the pattern.

Carve and model the design with graver's knife, spoon, and cup spatulas. Seal the parts together to form a single pattern. Warm and shape as shown.

CASTING

Measure the amount of silver needed for casting the pattern (p. 9). Invest the pattern (p. 10); heat and cast the invested pattern (p. 13).

FINISHING

Saw off the sprue pins (p. 89); anneal (p. 85), pickle (p. 87), and buff (p. 99). Texture (p. 89). Solder the joint and catch in place (p. 94). Clean, color with potassium sulfide solution (p. 97), and polish (p. 99). Rivet the pin stem in the joint (p. 94).

BROOCH DESIGN

BROOCH WITH
CARVED DESIGN

PATTERN OF WAX

Draw design. Make a tracing of the separate parts.

Lubricate a glass slab. Melt carving with blending wax. Pour on the glass. Let cool. Add more wax to form a $\frac{1}{8}$-inch wax sheet. Lay the tracings on the wax sheet. Pin prick the design into the wax. Remove the tracing and rub white powder over the wax surface. Dust off, leaving white powder in the pricked holes. Join the holes with a carved line. Repeat with white powder to form the outline of the design. Cut the outside outline with a knife spatula to release patterns. Form the design with warm spoon, cup and knife spatulas.

WAX PATTERN

Warm and bend to shape. Remove excess wax from the back to
make the casting lighter in weight.
Seal together to form a single pattern.

CASTING

Measure the amount of silver required. Warm the point of the
sprue pin and insert in the wax
pattern. Add extra sprues. Seal
the pin to the sprue former. Paint
with vacufilm.

Cover the wax surface with
mixed investment about ⅛ inch
thick. Do not let it dry before
filling the flask with investment.

Line the flask with damp asbestos
sheet. Seal the flask to the sprue
former. Fill the flask with mixed
investment. Remove the sprue
former and sprue pin when the investment has set. Pickle the metal
to be cast. Heat the flask in
the furnace. Prepare the crucible.
Cast the pattern.

CASTING

FINISHING

Saw off cast sprues. Anneal the
casting. Clean in pickle. Texture.
Solder the joint and catch in place.
Clean, color, and polish. Rivet the
pin-stem in the joint.

Brooch with carved design and coral beads (Project 6), derived from natural moss forms.

BROOCH WITH CARVED DESIGN AND CORAL BEADS

PREPARATION OF THE WAX PATTERN

Draw the design. Spread a thin film of microfilm on a glass slab. Melt carving wax with blending wax. Pour melted wax on the lubricated glass slab. Let cool. Pour more melted wax over it. Repeat to form a sheet ¼ inch thick. Spread melted carving wax over the surface with a spoon spatula. Transfer the design to the wax sheet with a scratch awl. Cut around the outline of the design to release the pattern from the sheet. Carve the design with a graver (p. 89). Model with a warm spatula. Warm and bend the pattern to the desired form. Remove excess wax from the back of the pattern to make the casting lighter in weight.

CASTING

Measure the amount of silver needed for the casting (p. 9). Invest the pattern (p. 10); heat and cast the invested pattern (p. 13).

FINISHING

Saw off the sprue pins (p. 89); anneal (p. 85), pickle (p. 87), and buff (p. 99). Make hooks of ¹⁄₁₆-inch flat silver wire for the number of beads to be mounted. Solder (p. 91) the hooks to the back of the brooch. Bind and solder the joint and catch in place (p. 94).

Cut 2 inch lengths of 18-guage silver wire (the same number as hooks). Melt the ends of the wire into balls (p. 80). Pickle (p. 87). Smooth the surface with felt buff, bristle buff, and tripoli (p. 99). Color with potassium sulfide solution (p. 97), and polish with rouge and cloth buff (p. 99). Thread the wire through the beads to the back of the brooch. Wind around the hooks. Press the hooks to hold the wire. Rivet the pin stem in the joint (p. 94).

PROJECT 6

BROOCH WITH
CARVED DESIGN
AND CORAL BEADS

PATTERN OF WAX

Draw the design. Lubricate a glass slab. Melt carving wax with blending wax. Pour on the glass slab to form a wax sheet. Let cool. Repeat until the sheet is $\frac{1}{4}$ inch in thickness. Melt carving wax and spread over the surface. Scratch the design on the wax. Cut the outside outline to release the wax pattern. Carve and model the design. Warm the pattern. Bend to the form desired.

WAX PATTERN

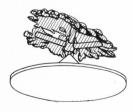

CASTING

CASTING

Measure the amount of silver required for casting. (Fig. 4) Seal the pattern to the sprue pin. Seal a $\frac{1}{4}$-inch wax ball $\frac{1}{16}$ inch from the pattern. Seal the sprue pin to the sprue former. Double the thickness of the pin between the pattern and the ball. Add extra sprues. Wash with water—use a soft brush or absorbent cotton. Paint with vacufilm. Let dry.

Paint the pattern and ball with mixed investment. Line the flask with damp asbestos sheet. Seal the flask to the sprue former. Fill the flask with mixed investment. Remove the sprue former and sprue pin when investment has set. Heat the flask. Prepare the crucible. Cast the pattern.

Finishing

Anneal the casting. Clean in pickle. Saw off cast sprues. Buff and polish. Make hooks of $\frac{1}{16}$-inch flat silver wire for the number of beads to be mounted. Solder the hooks to the back of the brooch. Cut 2-inch lengths of 18-gauge silver wire for number of hooks.

Melt the wire ends into balls. Bind and solder the joint and catch in place. Clean, color, and polish. Thread the wire ends through the beads to the back of the brooch. Wind the wire around the hooks. Press the hooks to hold the wire. Rivet the pin stem in the joint.

Finished brooch and natural motif, showing decorative use of silver balls
(Project 7).

BROOCH WITH SILVER BALLS AND LEAF

Preparation of the Wax Pattern

Draw the design. Trace the design for the foundation and leaf. Cut a paper pattern from the tracing. Warm sculpture wax. Mold and press wax on a lubricated glass slab to form a 16-gauge wax sheet. Lay the paper patterns on the wax sheet and cut around them with a knife.

To make wire, roll sculpture wax into 14-gauge wire (p. 81). Seal the wire to the foundation with the hot point of a needle. Flatten the top and sides slightly with a warm spatula.

To make balls, roll sculpture wax into 16-gauge wire (p. 81). Cut the wire into several lengths and roll into balls (p. 81). Warm the point of a large needle. Starting with the larger balls, melt a spot in the center of the foundation wire and seal the ball in the melted wax. Continue sealing on the balls, tapering to the ends, as shown.

Melt the edge of the foundation at an angle with a warm spatula. (The balls should cover the edge.) Press the wax into an 18-gauge sheet. Cut and seal the leaf to the foundation. Model and smooth the leaf and stems with a warm spatula. Remove excess wax from the back of the pattern with a warm spoon spatula, to make the casting lighter in weight.

Casting

Measure the amount of silver needed for casting the pattern (p. 9). Invest the pattern (p. 10); heat and cast the invested pattern (p. 13).

Finishing

Saw off the sprue pins (p. 89); anneal (p. 85), pickle (p. 87), and buff (p. 99). Bind and solder the joint and catch in place (p. 94). Pickle (p. 87), color with potassium sulfide solution (p. 97), and polish (p. 99). Rivet pin stem in the joint.

BROOCH WITH BALLS AND LEAF

PATTERN OF WAX

Draw the design. Cut paper patterns of foundation and leaf. Press and mold sculpture wax into a 16-gauge wax sheet. Cut the wax sheet to pattern to form foundation. Make a round wax wire, 14-gauge. Seal the wire to the foundation. Scrape the top and sides to flatten slightly. Make a round wire, 16-gauge. Cut and roll into balls in several sizes. Mold and press wax into 18-gauge wax sheet. Cut the leaf from the pattern. Melt a spot in the foundation wire. Seal a ball in the melted wax. Continue sealing balls, tapering to ends with smaller balls. Melt the edge of the foundation with a warm spatula. Seal the leaf to the foundation. Smooth the surface. Remove excess wax from the back.

Casting

Measure the amount of silver required for the casting. Mount the pattern on a sprue pin. Seal a ¼-inch ball ¹⁄₁₆ inch from the pattern. Double the thickness of the pin between the ball and the pattern. Add extra sprues as shown. Seal the sprue pin to the sprue former. Wash in water (use a soft brush or absorbent cotton). Paint with vacufilm. Let dry. Paint the pattern and wax ball with mixed investment ⅛ inch thick. (Do not let the investment dry completely before filling the flask.) Line the flask with damp asbestos sheet. Seal flask to sprue former. Fill the flask with mixed investment. Remove the sprue former and pin when the investment has set. Heat the flask in the furnace. Prepare the crucible. Cast the pattern.

CASTING

Finishing

Saw off the cast sprues. Anneal the casting. Clean in pickle. Bind and solder the joint and catch in place. Color and polish.

Brooch with carnelian stones, domes, and carved design (Project 8), and natural motif.

BROOCH WITH CARNELIAN STONES
AND CARVED DESIGN

PREPARATION OF THE WAX PATTERN

Draw the design. Trace the design. Saw a piece of Blue Karvex wax slightly larger than the tracing, and ¼ inch thick. Smooth with file and sandpaper. Lay the tracing on the wax surface and prick the design into the wax with the point of a needle. Rub white powder over the wax. Dust the surface, leaving white powder in the pricks. Follow the transfer with a pointed graver. Dust with white powder to leave a white line transfer of the design.

Place the stones in position on the wax. Scratch a line around the circumference of the stones allowing enough extra space to form the bezels. Carve the design; saw the openings in the design. Cut the wax under the sets to leave bearings. Make solid domes (p. 82) and seal in place. Remove excess wax from the back to make casting lighter in weight. Smooth all surfaces with a warm spatula. Wash in water, brushing with a soft brush or absorbent cotton.

CASTING

Measure the amount of silver needed for casting the pattern (p. 9). Invest the pattern (p. 10); heat and cast the invested pattern (p. 13).

FINISHING

Saw off the sprue pins (p. 89); anneal (p. 85), pickle (p. 87), and buff (p. 99). Texture (p. 89). Solder the joint and catch in place (p. 94). Color with potassium sulfide solution (p. 97) and polish (p. 99). Set the stones (p. 76). Rivet the pin stem in the joint.

PROJECT 8

BROOCH WITH CARNELIAN STONES, DOMES AND CARVED DESIGN

PATTERN OF WAX

Draw the design. Make a tracing. Saw Blue Karvex wax to fit the tracing, ¼ inch thick. Lay the tracing on the wax. Pin prick the design. Rub white powder over the wax surface. Dust to leave pin prick white tracing. Use a pointed graver to follow the transfer. Dust with white powder, leaving a white line. Place the stones in position on the wax. Scratch a line around the girdle of the stone. Add to the circumference to form the bezels. Carve as shown. Saw the center, leaving enough for the bearing. Carve the design. Saw the openings.

Make solid domes. Seal the domes in place.

WAX PATTERN

CASTING

Measure the amount of silver required. Wash in water. Use a soft brush or absorbent cotton. Warm the point of a sprue pin. Insert in the wax pattern. Add extra sprues of wax wire (as shown). Seal the pin to the sprue former. Paint with vacufilm or debubblizer. Line the flask with damp asbestos sheet $\frac{1}{4}$-inch from the rims and $\frac{1}{2}$-inch overlap. Cover the wax surface with mixed investment $\frac{1}{8}$ inch thick. Do not let it dry before the flask is filled. Seal the flask to the sprue former. Fill the flask with mixed investment. Remove the sprue former and sprue pin when the investment has set. Pickle the metal to be cast. Heat the flask in the furnace. Prepare the crucible. Cast the pattern. Anneal the casting.

CASTING

FINISHING

Saw off cast sprues. Clean in pickle. Texture. Solder joint and catch in place. Clean, color, and polish. Set the stones. Rivet the pin stem in the joint.

BROOCH WITH PEARLS AND CARVED DESIGN

PREPARATION OF THE WAX PATTERN

Draw the design. Trace the design. Place a chunk of soluble wax in the jaws of the table vise. Saw the wax with a hacksaw (p. 89) to form a flat surface slightly larger than the traced design and ½ inch thick. Smooth the surface with a file and sandpaper. Place carbon paper on the prepared surface. Transfer the traced design to the wax. Carve intaglio $\frac{3}{16}$ inch deep.

Spread microfilm on a glass slab. Place wax on the slab, carved side up. Melt carving wax with blending wax. Pour the melted wax over the carved surface. Let cool. Repeat to a thickness of 18-gauge. Place the wax in a bowl of cold water to dissolve the soluble wax, leaving the raised design on the 18-gauge sheet.

Lay the sheet with the raised design on the glass slab and cut around the design to release the pattern. Melt carving wax and spread over the pattern with a spoon spatula. Carve with a graver; model with a warm spatula. Warm the pattern and bend to form (as shown). Remove excess wax from the back of the pattern with a warm spoon spatula, to make the casting lighter in weight. Wash in water, brushing with a soft brush or absorbent cotton.

CASTING

Measure the amount of silver needed for casting the pattern (p. 9). Invest the pattern (p. 10); heat and cast the invested pattern (p. 13).

FINISHING

Saw off the sprue pins (p. 89); anneal (p. 85), pickle (p. 87), buff and polish (p. 99). Bind and solder the joint and catch in place (p. 94). Color with potassium sulfide solution (p. 97) and polish (p. 99). Rivet the pin stem in the joint. Hold the pearls in place with epoxy cement.

Segments of pine cones provided the motif for necklace or pendant, Project 13.

BROOCH DESIGN

BROOCH WITH
PEARLS AND
CARVED DESIGN

PATTERN OF WAX

Draw the design. Trace the drawing. Saw and smooth soluble wax—a piece slightly larger than the tracing, and $\frac{1}{2}$ inch thick. Transfer the tracing to the wax surface with carbon paper. Carve the design intaglio $\frac{3}{16}$ inch in depth. Lubricate a glass slab. Melt carving wax with blending wax. Pour over the carved surface to fill the carving and to form a wax sheet 18-gauge. Place in a bowl of cold water to dissolve the soluble wax, leaving the carved design. Cut the sheet around the design to release the pattern. Melt carving wax in a spoon spatula. Spread the melted wax over the pattern to form a carving surface. Carve and model (as shown). Remove excess wax from the back of the pattern to make the casting lighter in weight.

WAX PATTERN

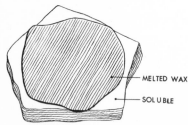

MELTED WAX

SOLUBLE

CASTING

Measure the amount of silver required for the casting. Warm the point of a sprue pin. Insert in the wax pattern. Add extra sprues of wax wire (as shown). Seal a ¼-inch ball ⅟₁₆ inch from the pattern. Double the thickness of the pin between the pattern and ball. Seal the sprue pin to the sprue former. Wash in water with a soft brush or absorbent cotton. Paint the wax surface with vacufilm. Line the flask with damp asbestos sheet. Cover the wax surface with mixed investment ⅛ inch thick. Do not let the investment dry before the flask is filled. Seal flask to the sprue former. Fill flask with mixed investment. Remove the sprue former and sprue pin when the investment has set. Pickle the metal to be cast. Heat the flask in the furnace. Prepare the crucible. Cast the pattern.

FINISHING

Saw off cast sprues. Anneal the casting. Clean in pickle. Solder the joint and catch in place. Clean, color, and polish. Rivet the pin stem in the joint. Hold the pearls in place with epoxy cement.

CASTING

Pendant with open work and carved design (Project 10) and natural motif.

PENDANT WITH OPENWORK AND CARVED DESIGN

PREPARATION OF THE WAX PATTERN

Draw the design. Place a piece of soluble wax in the jaws of the table vise and saw off a piece of wax with the hacksaw (p. 89) large enough to form a core. File and shape into an oval core. Place four pieces of 10-gauge half-round wax wire lengthwise around the core to form a frame. Seal the ends together. Seal 18-gauge round wax wire to the frame to form the vines. Draw the leaf design and place the drawing on a lubricated glass slab. Place pink casting wax over the drawing and cut the leaves with a knife. Seal the leaves to the vines and frame.

Melt balls on the ends of 14-gauge wax wire (p. 80). Seal the balls in place on the pattern, as shown. Melt carving wax. Spread over the frame, vines, and leaves with a spoon spatula to form a carving surface. Carve and model the leaves with a graver and warm spatula. Place the pattern in a bowl of cold water to dissolve the soluble wax.

CASTING

Measure the amount of silver needed for casting the pattern (p. 9). Invest the pattern (p. 10); heat and cast the invested pattern (p. 13).

FINISHING

Saw off the sprue pins (p. 89), leaving a short length at the top. File and bend to form a hook. Anneal (p. 85), pickle (p. 87), buff (p. 99), color with potassium sulfide solution (p. 97), and polish (p. 99).

PENDANT DESIGN

WAX PATTERN

PENDANT WITH OPENWORK AND CARVED DESIGN

Pattern of wax

Draw the design. Saw a piece of soluble wax. File and shape to form a core. Seal 10-gauge half-round wire lengthwise around the core. Seal 18-gauge round wire to the 10-gauge wire to form a vine. Draw the leaf design. Place pink casting wax over the drawing. Cut the leaves. Seal the leaves to the vine. Make balls of 14-gauge wire. Seal in place (as shown). Melt carving wax. Spread over the leaves and wires. Carve and model. Place the pattern in cold water to dissolve the soluble wax.

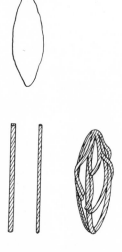

CASTING

Measure the amount of silver required for the casting. Mount the pattern on a sprue pin. Seal a ¼-inch wax ball $\frac{1}{16}$ inch from the pattern. Double the thickness of the pin between the pattern and the ball. Seal the sprue pin to the sprue former. Add extra sprues. Wash in water—use a soft brush or absorbent cotton. Paint with vacufilm. Let dry. Paint the pattern and ball with mixed investment. Line the flask with damp asbestos sheet. Seal the flask to the sprue former. Fill the flask with mixed investment before the invested pattern is completely dry. Remove the sprue former and pin when the investment has set. Heat the flask. Prepare the crucible. Cast the pattern.

CASTING

FINISHING

Saw off the cast sprues. Anneal the casting. Clean in pickle. Leaving a short length at the top, file and bend to form the hook. Carve and texture the leaves. Color and polish.

OWL PENDANT

Preparation of the wax pattern

Draw the design. Cut a paper pattern. Spread a thin film of microfilm on a glass slab. Melt carving wax with blending wax and pour on the lubricated surface. Let cool. Pour more melted wax over it and repeat to form a wax sheet 10-gauge thick. Cut the pattern from the wax sheet and an opening slightly smaller than the base of the stone.

Place the stone on a flat surface. Warm the pattern and place the opening over the stone. Shape and model. Lubricate a large dapping die punch. Place the pattern on the dapping die block, the head of the bird on the die the size of the punch. Press into the die to raise the head.

Melt carving wax and spread over the pattern with a spoon spatula. Warm a small dapping die punch and press into the pattern to form the eye sockets. Make two balls (p. 80) and seal in place for the eyes. Seal a lump of wax in place for the beak. Carve and model.

Seal two lengths of 10-gauge half-round wax wire together. Cut and shape six pieces of 14-gauge half-round wax wire. Seal to the 10-gauge wire and to the pattern. Cut four lengths of 10-gauge sheet wax for sprues (p. 8). Seal to the back of the pattern. Leave parts unsealed at the edge of the opening to insert and hold the stone when part of the sprues have been sawed off.

Casting

Measure the amount of silver needed for casting the pattern (p. 9). Invest the pattern (p. 10); heat and cast the invested pattern (p. 13).

FINISHING

Saw off sprues (p. 89) leaving ends to hold the stone. File and shape ends. Anneal (p. 85), pickle (p. 87), carve and texture (p. 89), color with potassium sulfide solution (p. 97), and polish (p. 99). Set stone (p. 76) and burnish the sprue ends over the stone.

OWL PENDANT WITH AGATE STONE AND CARVED DESIGN

PATTERN OF WAX

Draw the design. Cut a paper pattern. Lubricate a glass slab. Melt carving wax with blending wax. Pour on the slab to form a sheet. Let cool. Repeat to form a 10-gauge wax sheet.

Finished owl pendant.

PENDANT DESIGN

WAX PATTERN

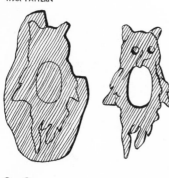

Cut the pattern from the wax sheet. Cut an opening slightly smaller than the stone. Warm the pattern and place the opening over the stone. Shape and model the contour of the stone. Lubricate a large dapping die punch. Warm the pattern and place the head on the dapping die block, the die the size of the punch. Press and model. Melt carving wax and spread over the head, wings, and tail. Form the eye sockets with a small dapping die punch. Seal a lump of wax in place for the beak.

Make two balls and seal in place. Cut two pieces of 10-gauge half-round wax wire. Seal together and shape to form branch. Cut six lengths of 14-gauge half-round wax wire. Bend and seal in pairs to form the claws. Seal to the branch. Seal the branch in place. Carve and model the pattern.

Cut four lengths from 10-gauge wax sheet ⅛ inch in width, one wide enough at one end to form the tail feathers, another for hook. Seal to the back of the pattern to form sprues. Leave enough unsealed to insert the stone and hold from the back. Remove excess wax from the back of the pattern.

CASTING

Measure the amount of silver required for the casting. Mount the pattern on the sprue pin. Seal a ¼-inch wax ball $\frac{1}{16}$ inch from the pattern. Double the thickness of the pin between pattern and ball. Seal the sprue pin to the sprue former. Wash in water; paint with vacufilm.

Line the flask with damp asbestos sheet. Cover the pattern and wax ball with mixed investment ⅛ inch thick. Do not let dry before the flask is filled with investment. Seal the flask to the sprue former. Fill the flask with mixed investment. Remove the sprue former and sprue pin when the investment has set. Heat the flask in the furnace. Prepare the crucible. Cast the pattern.

FINISHING

Saw off sprue pins, leaving enough to hold the stone. File the ends to lighter gauge. Anneal the casting; pickle; carve and texture the casting. Buff, color, and polish. Set the stone. Make a hook of silver wire. Solder hook and catch. Rivet the pin stem in the joint.

CASTING

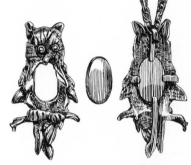

BOLA TIE SLIDE WITH
STONE AND CARVED DESIGN

PREPARATION OF THE WAX PATTERN

Draw the design. Cut a paper pattern. Spread a thin film of microfilm on a glass slab. Melt carving wax with blending wax and pour on the glass slab. Let cool. Add more melted wax to form a 10-gauge sheet. Place the paper pattern on the wax sheet. Cut around the outline with a knife spatula to release the pattern.

Lubricate the stone. Warm the wax sheet. Place the stone in position and press into the warm wax. Remove the stone. Carve to form a deeper depression. Cut out the impression in the wax made by the stone to leave a bearing for the stone to rest upon. Replace the stone in the wax. Add melted carving wax with a spoon spatula to form the face and headdress. Carve and model. Make balls (p. 80) for the eyes and seal in place. Remove excess wax from the back to make the casting lighter in weight.

CASTING

Measure the amount of silver needed for casting the pattern (p. 9). Invest the pattern (p. 10); heat and cast the invested pattern (p. 13).

FINISHING

Saw off the sprue pins (p. 89), leaving a short length to form a hook. File and shape hook. Cut a length of 14-gauge silver wire. Make a ring on each end of the wire to fit the leather tie. Hold to the back of the pendant with the hook. Make a round coil of 18-gauge silver wire to fit the leather ends of the tie. Texture the headdress (p. 89). Smooth the surface with felt buff, bristle buff, and tripoli (p. 99). Color with potassium sulfide solution (p. 97), and polish (p. 99) with rouge and soft cloth buff. Insert the two ends of the tie through the rings held by the hook and into the two coils. Place a black bead on the ends of the coils and hold in place with epoxy cement.

> NOTE: Water-washed pebbles often take a high temperature and may be cast in the mold without cracking. The one for this bola tie (shown here) is black and in the shape of a head. Many times the shape of the pebble suggests the design.
>
> Before combining the stone with the wax for the burn-out to form the mold, test a pebble under high heat, about 1200° F.
>
> When used in the pattern, weigh the stone before it is set in the wax pattern (Figs. 3 and 4) to determine the amount of silver to be cast.

Bola tie slide and water-washed pebble used for the face (Project 12).

SLIDE DESIGN

BOLA TIE SLIDE
WITH STONE AND
CARVED DESIGN

PATTERN OF WAX

Draw the design. Cut a paper pattern. Lubricate a glass slab. Melt carving wax with blending wax. Pour on the glass slab. Let cool. Add more melted wax to form a 10-gauge sheet. Lubricate the stone and press into the warm wax. Remove the stone. Carve the wax to form a deeper depression. Cut the center, leaving a rim for the bearing. Lay the paper pattern on the wax sheet. Cut the outside outline of the design.

WAX PATTERN

CASTING

Measure the amount of silver required for the casting. Replace the stone. Add melted carving wax with a spoon spatula to form the face and headdress. Carve and model as shown. Make two balls for the eyes. Seal the balls in place. Remove excess wax from the back of the pattern.

Mount the pattern on a sprue pin. Seal a $\frac{1}{4}$-inch ball $\frac{1}{16}$ inch from the pattern. Double the thickness of the pin between the

pattern and ball. Add extra sprues.
Seal the sprue pin to the sprue
former. Wash in water, using a
soft brush or absorbent cotton.
Paint with vacufilm.

Line the flask with damp asbestos sheet. Cover the wax pattern and stone with mixed investment ⅛-inch thick. Do not let
dry before filling the flask with
investment. Seal the flask to the
sprue former. Fill the flask with
mixed investment. Remove the
sprue former and sprue pin when
the investment has set. Pickle the
metal to be cast. Heat the flask
in the furnace. Prepare the crucible. Cast the pattern.

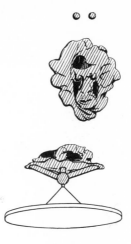

CASTING

FINISHING

Saw off extra sprues. Leave a
short length on top sprue to form a
hook (as shown). Clean in pickle.
Texture the headdress. Cut a
length of 14-gauge wire. Make
two rings on each end to fit the
leather tie. Hold to the back with
the hook. Coil 18-gauge wire to
fit the leather ends. Cement black
ceramic beads on the ends with
epoxy cement.

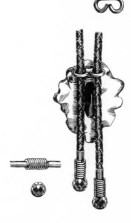

PENDANT OR NECKLACE OF CARVED UNITS

PREPARATION OF THE WAX PATTERN

To make a single unit:

Draw the design. Trace the design. Saw a piece of Blue Karvex wax slightly larger than the drawing. Smooth the surface with file and sandpaper. Lay the tracing on the wax surface and prick the design into the wax with the point of a needle. Rub white powder over the wax. Dust the surface, leaving white powder in the holes. Join the holes with a carved line. Dust again with white powder. Saw along the outline of the transfer to release the pattern. Model the unit with file, graver, and warm spatula. Remove excess wax from the back of the unit to make casting lighter in weight.

CASTING

Measure the amount of silver needed for casting the pattern (p. 9). Invest the pattern (p. 10); heat and cast the invested pattern (p. 13).

FINISHING

Saw off the sprue pins (p. 89); anneal (p. 85), pickle (p. 87). Make a hook of $\frac{1}{8}$-inch flat silver wire. Solder in place (p. 91). Buff (p. 99), color (p. 97), and polish (p. 99).

> NOTE: This unit may be hooked by itself to a chain as a pendant or several units may be attached to a chain in graduated series to form a necklace.

To make several units:

Spread a thin film of microfilm on a glass slab. Mix together equal parts from the two tubes of Regular Permlastic material. Place the mixture on the glass slab and form a block about $\frac{1}{2}$ inch thick and larger than the die (using the above single unit pattern as die). Lubricate the die and press into the prepared block to form a mold.

Melt carving wax with blending wax. Pour the melted wax into the mold. Remove the wax pattern when cool. Smooth the edges and refine the carved lines. Remove excess wax from the back of the pattern to make the casting lighter in weight.

Pour melted wax in the same mold to form more wax patterns, as many as you will need for the necklace. To graduate the units, lay the patterns on a glass slab and trim down the edges with a knife spatula to reduce the size. Smooth with a warm spatula.

Cast and finish as described above. Several patterns may be mounted on the same sprue former, the number depending upon the size of the flask.

DIE AND MOLD

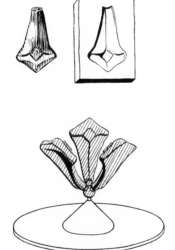

UNIT DESIGN

UNIT WITH CARVED DESIGN

PATTERN OF WAX

Draw the design. Make a tracing. Saw a piece of Karvex wax ¼-inch thick, slightly larger than the tracing. Smooth the wax surface. Lay the tracing on the wax. Pin prick the tracing into the wax. Remove the tracing. Rub white powder over the wax surface. Dust leaving outline in white pin pricks. Join the transfer with a carved line. Rub white powder again on the wax. Dust off to leave white line of the design. Saw the outside outline. File and carve (as shown). Remove excess wax from the back to make the casting lighter in weight.

WAX PATTERN

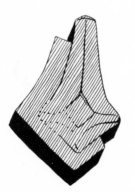

Casting

Measure the amount of silver to be cast. Insert the warm end of the sprue pin in the end of the unit, seal with wax. Place a ¼-inch ball on the sprue pin ⅛ inch from the pattern. Double the thickness of the pin between pattern and ball. Seal the pin to the sprue former. Wash in water with a soft brush or absorbent cotton.

Line the flask with damp asbestos ¼ inch from rims and ½-inch overlap. Paint the wax surface with vacufilm. Cover with mixed investment. Seal the flask to the sprue former. Fill the flask with mixed investment before the invested pattern is completely dry. Remove the sprue former and sprue pin when the investment has set. Heat the flask in the furnace. Prepare the crucible. Cast the pattern.

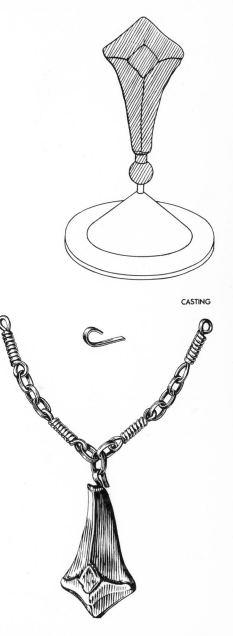

CASTING

Finishing

Anneal the casting. Clean in pickle. Saw off cast sprue pin. Make a hook of ⅛ inch in width of flat wire. Solder in place. Buff, color, and polish.

Earrings designed from acorns (Project 14) showing use of domes and balls.

EARRINGS WITH DOMES AND CARNELIAN BEADS

Preparation of the wax pattern

Draw the design. Melt carving wax with blending wax in a small container several inches in depth. Select a dapping die punch the size of the bead. Lubricate the punch with microfilm. Hold the punch perpendicular and dip in the melted wax. Remove and cool. Repeat to form a heavier gauge. Let the wax form at the base of the dome (as shown). Cut the dome from the punch while the wax is warm. Repeat to form four domes.

Seal the domes together in pairs with wax wire, 10-gauge, half-round. Smooth and model the wax surface with a warm spatula. Wash the pattern in cold water with a soft brush or absorbent cotton.

Casting

Measure the amount of silver needed for casting the pattern (p. 9). Invest the pattern (p. 10); heat and cast the invested pattern (p. 13).

Finishing

Saw off the sprue pins (p. 89); anneal (p. 85), pickle (p. 87), texture (p. 89). Solder ear screws in place with soft solder (p. 91). Color (p. 97), polish and buff (p. 99).

Cut four lengths of 18-gauge silver wire and melt a ball on each wire end (as wax wire ball, p. 80). Paint the wires with epoxy cement and insert the ends in each bead. Let dry. Cut the wire ends even with the beads. Paint the insides of the domes with epoxy cement and place the beads in the domes.

EARRING DESIGN

EARRINGS WITH DOMES AND CARNELIAN BEADS

Pattern of Wax

Draw the design. Melt carving wax with blending wax. Select a dapping die punch the size of the bead. Lubricate the punch with microfilm. Dip the punch in the hot wax to form a dome. Hold the punch perpendicular. Remove from the melted wax. Let cool. Dip again in the wax. Cut the wax from the punch while warm to release the dome. Repeat the above to form four domes. Wax wire, 10-gauge, half round. Seal the domes together in pairs with the wire. Smooth and model with warm spatula.

WAX PATTERN

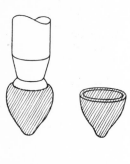

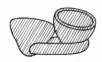

Casting

Measure the amount of silver required for the casting. Mount

the patterns on a sprue pin. Seal a
$\frac{1}{4}$-inch wax ball $\frac{1}{16}$ inch from
the patterns. Double the thickness
of the pin between the pattern and
the ball. Seal the sprue pin to the
sprue former. Wash in water—use
a soft brush. Paint with vacufilm.
Let dry. Line the flask with damp
asbestos sheet. Cover the wax surface $\frac{1}{8}$ inch thick with mixed investment. Seal the flask to the
sprue former base. Fill the flask
with mixed investment before the
invested pattern is completely dry.
Remove the sprue former and pin
when the investment has set. Heat
the flask. Prepare the crucible.
Cast the pattern.

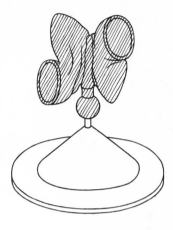

CASTING

FINISHING

Saw off cast sprue. Anneal the
casting. Clean in pickle. Texture
the casting. Solder ear screws in
place with soft solder. Color, polish, and buff. Cut four lengths
silver wire, 18-gauge. Melt a ball
on each wire end. Paint the wire
with epoxy cement. Insert a wire
in each bead. Let dry. Cut wire
ends even with the beads. Paint
the inside of the domes with epoxy
cement. Place the beads in the
domes.

III.   DECORATIVE PROCESSES

Stone Setting
Wire Working, Balls, and Domes

DECORATIVE PROCESSES

STONE SETTING

Stones are set in jewelry to add color and luster. Either the stone is selected to suit the design or the article has been designed to fit around the stone, thus making the setting and the design a single unit. The method to be used for settings is determined by the shape and cut of the stone and by the construction and design of the article. Some of the settings are held by a collar of metal, called a bezel, which fits around the circumference of the stone and is tapped and burnished over the edge of the stone. Claws or prongs may also hold the stone in place; or a paved, sometimes called a gypsy, setting is recessed and the edge filed and burnished over the edge of the stone to blend with the surface contour. Small stones may be glued in the bezel with epoxy cement. Stones are set *after* the article has been cleaned, colored, and buffed to avoid scratching or discoloring the stone.

Measuring the circumference of a cabachon stone

Make a loop of 26-gauge binding wire. Run the two ends of the wire into the holes of the dentemeter. Place the stone in the loop. Twist the wire until it fits the girdle of the stone. Cut the loop in the center. Spread the ends to determine the circumference (Fig. 7).

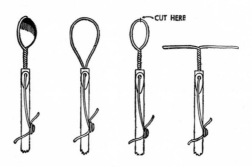

Fig. 7. Measuring the girdle of a stone with the dentimetre and binding wire.

Setting the stone

Hold the article on a shellac stick or ring clamp (Fig. 8) depending upon the size and shape of the article. Place the tool selected to hold the article in the jaws of the table vice. Place the stone in the set with the stone lifter. (A stone lifter is made by heating and modeling a small piece of dental sticky wax on a stick; warm the wax slightly and press firmly on the top of the stone.) Be sure the girdle of the stone rests on the bearing. Tap the metal around and over the edge of the stone with a small repoussé tool and chasing hammer, as shown. Smooth with a file and graver; burnish the metal thus hammered with a burnisher.

Retouch color with a small brush. Rub with a chamois cloth or buffing wheel for the final polish. A burnisher may also be used.

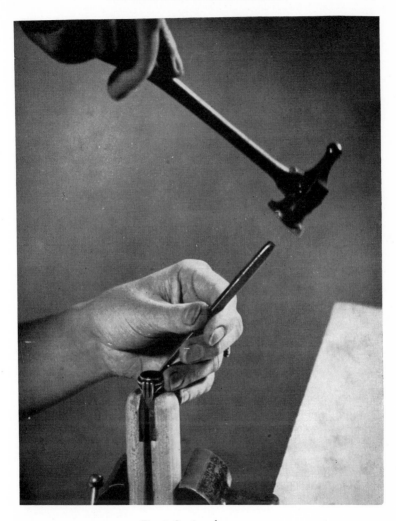

Fig. 8. Setting the stone.

Paved or gypsy setting

This type of setting (Fig. 9) is made in the wax pattern to form a recess the exact size of the girdle of the stone and a base on which it may rest. It may be formed by pressing a cabachon stone with a flat base into warm wax, or it may be carved in hard wax. Enough wax must be left above the bearing for the casting to be tapped and burnished over the stone to hold it in place. The thickness of the metal of the upper edge should be filed at an angle so the burnished edge will mold over and blend with the surface of the stone.

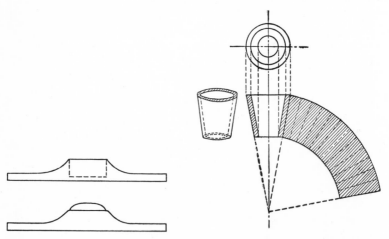

Fig. 9. Paved or gypsy setting.   Fig. 10. Pattern for a frustum of a hollow cone.

Bezel with bearing or claw setting
for a round cut stone

To make the frustum of a hollow cone, measure the circumference of the stone, and from the base or point of the stone to the girdle (Fig. 10). Add enough to this measurement to allow for burnishing over the edge of the stone.

Melt carving wax with blending wax. Pour on a lubricated glass slab to form a wax sheet. Make a paper pattern of the frustum (Fig. 10), lay it on the wax sheet, and cut the pattern from the sheet. Shape and seal the joint. The bearing for this type of setting may be carved or set in.

When the pattern has been cast and the stone set, the bezel is burnished over the edge of the stone. It may also be filed to form prongs to hold the stone in place. Or half-round wax wire may be sealed to the pattern to form claws; then when cast, they are filed and bent to hold the stone.

WIRE WORKING, BALLS, AND DOMES

Smooth and twisted wire, balls, and domes are often used for added ornamentation. The broken edge of a twisted wire gives a light and dark effect and a feeling of delicacy; balls and domes lend weight and luster to a design. These can be made from prepared wax shapes or can be fashioned out of sculpture wax on a glass slab.

Wax shapes in smooth wire form come in several gauges: round, half-round, soft, and flexible. Such decorative ornaments as coiled motifs and balls or the foundation for a brooch or pendant may be made from smooth or twisted wire. Sculpture wax is soft enough to be rolled easily into round wire and balls but, for twists and coils, it is not as good as the prepared wax shapes which hold their forms better.

Processes for making these ornamental shapes are given on the following pages.

TWISTED WIRE

ROUND TWIST:

Three sizes: 18-, 16-, 14-gauge round wire.

Two wires of equal length held parallel and together at both ends and twisted.

FLAT OPEN TWIST:

16-gauge round wire.

Two wires given a loose twist, pressed flat on a hard surface.

OPEN TWIST:

10-gauge half-round wire.
One wire given a loose twist.

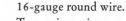

BALLS

BALLS ON WIRE ENDS:

14- and 16-gauge round wire.

Hold the wire as shown over an alcohol flame. Let the end melt slowly. Move with care away from the heat when the ball has formed.

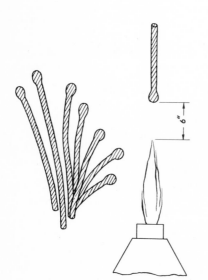

COILED WIRE

FLAT WIRE COILS (see opposite)

14- or 16-gauge round wire.
1. *The jig:* Cut a disk of heavy smooth cardboard. Punch a center hole the size of the mandrel. Notch one side of the hole. Mount the jig as shown. Place in the jaws of the table vice.

Coiling: Make a coil around the mandrel; press flat. Each coil should touch the one just formed. Cut the holding end. The coil may be spread to be more open.

2. *The jig:* Space the nails and hammer in a wooden block.

Coiling: Coil the wire as shown. Seal the beginning end under the first loop.

SCULPTURE WAX WIRE

⅛-inch sculpture wax sheet.

ROUND WIRE:

Take two glass slabs. Warm one and lay on the bench. Cut a strip of wax ⅛-inch in width. Mold in the hands to flatten edges. Rotate the strip between the glass slabs.

TAPERED END:

Rotate and move the glass slab over part of the wire slowly to the end.

BALLS:

Cut a small piece of wire. Press the ends together. Roll in the palm of the hand and on the glass.

BALL WITH CENTER DEPRESSION:

Make a large ball of wax. Place the ball in the dapping die block slightly larger than the ball. Dip the dapping die punch in microfilm. Press into center of ball.

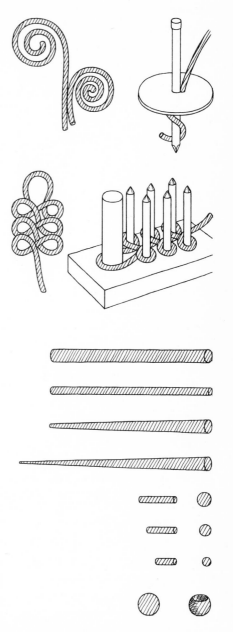

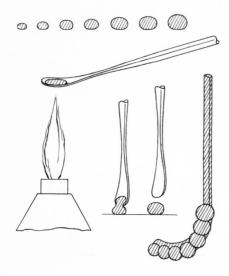

SOLID DOMES

KARVEX—Green or Blue

Spread microfilm on a glass slab. Heat a spoon spatula. Remove enough wax from the Karvex block to fill the spoon. Heat the wax over an alcohol flame. Hold the spatula over a glass sheet as shown. Touch the ball as it forms on the tip of the spatula to a glass surface. Withdraw the spatula slowly, leaving a small solid dome resembling a ball when mounted.

HOLLOW DOMES

Casting wax sheets 22-gauge, pink or green.

Dip dapping die punch and cutter in microfilm. Place casting sheet on a glass slab. Press the cutter on the wax to cut the disk. Place in the dapping die block the size of the disk. Press the punch smaller than the disk to form the hollow dome.

HOLLOW DOME
OR CUP

Melt hard carving and soft blending wax together. Lubricate a dapping die punch. Dip in the hot wax. Let cool and repeat the dip several times. Cut around the warm dome. Remove the cup (which also forms a hollow dome).

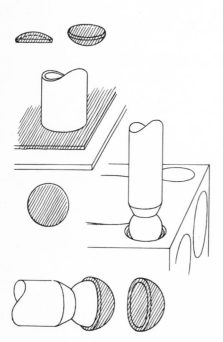

IV.   WORKING AND FINISHING PROCESSES

Annealing
Pickling
Texturing
Sawing
Filing
Soldering
Cleaning, Coloring, and Polishing

WORKING AND FINISHING PROCESSES

ANNEALING

Annealing is the process of heating metal to soften it and render it more pliable and easier to work. The number of times an article has to be annealed depends upon the amount of rolling, hammering, twisting, bending, and drawing to be done. These processes invariably harden metal and, in order to keep it sufficiently pliable to be worked, annealing may have to be done frequently in the course of construction. The amount and intensity of heat to be used depends upon the area and thickness of the piece to be annealed and upon the heat-retaining qualities of the surface on which the metal rests while heat is applied (Fig. 11). The distribution of the heat is important in annealing and the worker must learn how to keep the flame spread evenly until the whole piece turns a glowing red. It is the heat which renders the metal pliable.

Fig. 11. Annealing the metal with the blow torch flame.

TOOLS AND WORKING MATERIALS

Charcoal block
Asbestos pad
Annealing pan and charcoal
Gas and air blow torch
Iron binding wire 22-gauge

Snub nose pliers
Jeweler's shears
Sheet iron 26-gauge, 2 pieces
    about 4 inches square

PROCEDURE

Lay the metal to be annealed on the charcoal block. If the piece is large, use an asbestos pad or annealing pan and charcoal. Start with a loose flame, the size depending upon the gauge and size of the piece to be annealed. Keep the flame moving. Remove the flame when every section of the metal has become a glowing red. Cool by immersing the piece in water or pickle or let stand until cold enough to handle. *Gold 14K or under should not be immersed.*

PICKLING

Pickling is the most satisfactory way to clean a working surface. Metal oxidizes when it is exposed to the air and during all processes that require much heat. The coat of oxide must be removed as a clean surface is essential especially for soldering. (Borax glaze may also be removed by pickling; scale is removed with a fine emery cloth.) Boiling the metal in the pickle is the most effective method of cleaning metal, although plunging the hot metal into the pickle is also effective and simpler, particularly during the annealing process.

Pickling is used frequently during the construction of an article, and also before finishing and buffing. Sulfuric acid, nitric acid, and Sparex are used for pickles.

TOOLS AND WORKING MATERIALS

Sulfuric acid, for silver,
  copper, and gold
Sparex No. 2, for silver
  and copper
Nitric acid, for gold
  (14K and over)
Soda, ammonia, water solution

Deep earthenware pitcher
Porcelain pan
Granite pan
Copper pan
Copper tongs
Gas plate

Sulfuric formula: 1 sulfuric acid to 8–10 water. Heat in copper pan.

Sparex formula: 1½ pounds Sparex to 7 pints of lukewarm water (not over 125 degrees F.). Add Sparex slowly to lukewarm water. Stir until completely dissolved. Heat in copper pan.

> NOTE: Sparex is listed in jewelry supply catalogues and also sold in craft supply shops. Full directions for preparing and storing may be found on the package.

Nitric formula: 1 nitric acid to 8 water. Heat in porcelain pan.

When mixing acid, always pour the acid into the water, mixing it in a deep earthenware pitcher, to avoid splashing. Acid burns. A quart or more of pickle may be mixed at a time. It may be prepared in advance and stored for future use in a porcelain or earthenware container. Keep the pickle pan free of pickle when not in use.

PROCEDURE

Remove all binding wires. Pickle reacts on binding wire and discolors silver and gold. However, this film of discoloration is thin and may be removed by buffing.

Place the article to be cleaned in the pan and pour enough pickle into the pan to cover the article. Place the pan on the burner. Heating the pickle will increase the speed of the cleaning action. Boil the article in the pickle until pure white, if silver; self-color, if gold.

Remove the article from the pickle with copper tongs. Rinse thoroughly in cold water. Wash thoroughly in hot water. Boil

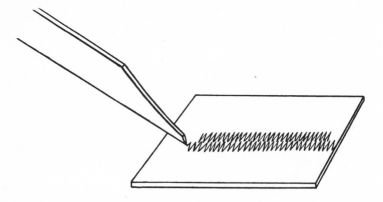

Fig. 12. Texturing with a flat graver.

in a strong solution of soda, ammonia, and water if there are recessed parts.

Follow this same procedure for all metals, all pickle solutions.

TEXTURING

Hold a flat graver at an angle on the metal. Press and move from right to left, removing small flakes of metal. This will leave a pattern when colored depth and contrast are desired in the design.

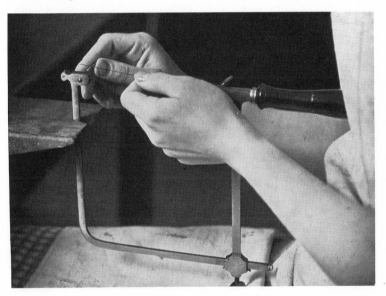

Fig. 13. Setting the saw blade.

SAWING

Sawing is cutting metal to a line. The jeweler's saw consists of an adjustable metal frame into which fine saw blades are fitted. Blades used for gold and silver 18-gauge and lighter are numbered 1/0 through 8/0. Heavier blades for heavier gauges are numbered 1, 2, etc.

Place the upper arm of the saw frame in the V of the bench pin. Hold the handle of the frame against the body as shown in Fig. 13. Fasten the blade in the jaw of the saw frame nearest the handle; the teeth must point *away* from the saw frame and *down* toward the handle. Press the saw frame thus held to shorten the span about ¼ inch. Place the loose end of the saw blade in the upper jaw of the saw frame; tighten the thumb screw.

Grasp the handle of the saw frame firmly with the little finger and thumb and hold the other three fingers loosely on the handle. Place the saw blade at right angles to the edge to be sawed. *Saw away* from the worker; make each stroke the length of the saw blade; the blade should not be pressed too firmly against the metal. Move the forearm up and down while sawing. Keep the back of the saw frame in a vertical position.

FILING

Excess metal, rough edges, and irregular surfaces are cut away or removed by filing. The types of files most commonly used in jewelry making are needle files in assorted shapes— half round, flat taper, triangular knife, and rat tail. Other files, four or six inches in length, second, and smooth cut, half round, triangular, flat riffle, and barrette are also used in jewelry construction and finishing. The cut refers to the teeth, whether single, double, or rasp cut, and to the fineness of the teeth.

The technique to be used for filing depends upon the condition of the metal, the type of surfaces or edges to be produced, and the file selected. The strokes should blend with and keep the contour or the shape of the line or form.

Any sawed or cut edge or clean surface can be filed without

being pickled. An annealed or soldered surface to be filed for construction practically always requires cleaning in the pickle to remove the oxidation or the borax glaze. The latter is difficult and sometimes impossible to remove with a file.

PROCEDURE

Place the pressure on the forward stroke of the file; remove the pressure on the return stroke. Pressure on the back stroke wears off the points of the teeth of the file. Remove the burr which remains on the metal after filing with a file, scraper, or emery cloth.

Clean the file at intervals with a file card or brush. Rub finer files over the rough surface of cloth.

SOLDERING

The purpose of soldering is to hold pieces of metal together. In all soldering, flux, solder, and heat are necessary, and binding is often essential to insure a close fit.

Binding wire comes in many gauges; number 28 or 32 for fine work, 24 or 26 for medium weight metal, 20 or 22 for heavier work. 12-, 14-, or 18-gauge wire may be rolled flat to make pins or clamps. Fine wire can be twisted evenly to make it heavier and still flexible.

Different qualities of solder used for jewelry—hard, medium, and easy-flowing—melt at different temperatures depending upon the kind and amount of alloy used. Hard solders contain alloys different from those used for soft solder. Hard solder is used to solder gold and silver jewelry and larger pieces of silverware. Silver solder should be used when soldering silver and gold together.

There are many prepared fluxes which can be purchased at a jeweler's supply store, though you can prepare a flux of borax and water yourself.

Tools and working materials

Prepared flux	Binding wire
Dividers	Blow torch
Jeweler's shears	Camel's hair brush
Charcoal block	Solder—hard, medium, easy-flowing

Procedure

Remove dirt and tarnish from the solder with a scraper or file. Scratch lines on the solder sheet $\frac{1}{16}$ inch apart. Cut across the lines as shown in Figure 14. Hold the solder be-

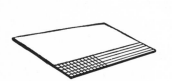

Fig. 14. Solder marked for cutting.

Fig. 15. Charcoal block used
when soldering and annealing.

tween the thumb and first finger. Let the ball of the second finger rest under the cut edge. Now cut along the scratched lines, at right angles to the first cuts made. Place the small pieces of cut solder on the edge of a saucer.

Pickle the metal to be soldered (see p. 87) and after each soldering; the surface must be kept clean because dirt and oxidation interfere with the flow of the solder. Wash thoroughly in water. Paint the metal with flux to exclude the air and to prevent heat from forming oxides on the metal.

Place the pieces to be joined by soldering on the charcoal block (Fig. 15). Be sure the surfaces to be joined touch each other at all points. Bind pieces together, if necessary, with annealed binding wire. (Sometimes the metal expands first and is cut by the wire; make Z-shaped kinks in the wire to avoid cutting.)

Apply the flux with a small camel's hair brush to the parts to be soldered. Dampen the brush and pick up the small pieces of solder on the saucer with the point of the brush. Place the bits of solder so that they touch the pieces of metal to be united.

Light the blow torch. The size of the flame to be used depends upon the weight of the metal to be united or the area to be heated or both. Apply the heat gradually to the parts to be united, if possible on the opposite side from where the solder is placed so that the solder will be drawn toward the joint rather than away from it.

Allow the moisture in the flux to evaporate as the flux will crystallize and hold the solder in place; flux covers and protects the surface from oxidation. Sometimes it is better to warm the surface and evaporate the moisure from the flux before applying the solder.

Heat the article so that all parts will become hot at the same time as solder in liquid form runs to the hottest part. The flame should be kept moving over the whole piece until it becomes a dull red. As the heat is applied, move the torch away from the metal now and then to see if any part is getting overheated; overheated solder eats into the metal. An overheated part will show at once by its glow. When the whole piece is sufficiently hot, direct the flame on the joint and melt the solder quickly so that it runs and joins all parts firmly together; solder becomes solid almost immediately when the heat is removed. Sometimes the solder will roll into a ball and not melt. When this happens a hotter flame is required and sometimes more flux should be applied. Sometimes this happens because oil and grease may not have been removed from the metal. If this is the case, pickle the metal and begin again.

Apply more solder dipped in flux to the joint with tweezers during the soldering process if necessary. Examine the joint. Apply more flux and heat if the solder has not melted.

To join a small piece to a large piece: In soldering a small piece of metal on a larger or heavier piece, place the larger piece on the charcoal block when possible. Direct the flame on the larger piece. The heat from the larger piece often heats the smaller piece sufficiently so that both pieces become hot at the same time, which is important. Direct a blast of heat on the smaller part when the larger part has reached a dull red to bring both pieces to the same temperature at the same time.

Joining a catch to a brooch: Place the right side of the brooch on the charcoal block—the top away from the worker. Care must be taken to keep a geometrical design or balanced design straight. Place the joint a little above the center on the right side of the back close to the outer edge. Place the catch directly opposite the joint with the opening down. Bind the joint and catch in place. Apply flux to both and warm slightly. Add small pieces of easy solder on one side of the catch and joint. Proceed as described in section on joining a small piece to a larger piece. When the joint and catch have been soldered in place, insert the wires which are in the pin stem through the holes in the joint. Press the ends with pliers.

SOLDERS AND FLUXES—TYPES AND USES

METALS	FLUX	SOLDER
Silver to Silver Fine or Sterling	Anti borax flux and water 1 tablespoon 2 oz. water—dissolved Borax—prepared in sticks or cones Rubbed on slate with water Other fluxes for hard solder are available	Medium-flowing silver solder for a general use Hard-flowing silver solder for (a) Built-up pieces which are heated many times (b) Pieces made of metal heavy enough to withstand much heat Easy-flowing silver solder for (a) Final soldering on certain types of built-up pieces (b) Delicate and light-weight pieces
Silver soldered to Gold	Fluxes as indicated	Silver solder as above
Gold soldered to Gold	Fluxes as indicated above	Gold solder the color of the gold
Silver soldered to Copper	Borax in any form used thick	Silver solder as above
Copper soldered to Copper	Borax in any form used thick	Silver solder as above
Tin to Tin	Zinc chloride one part, water one part Other fluxes for soft solder are available	Lead and tin solder

CLEANING, COLORING, AND POLISHING

Cleaning, and coloring, and polishing play a distinct part in the creation of a piece of jewelry. Cleaning is the basis of a good finish since no amount of coloring or polishing will cover up or remove scratches or excess solder. Coloring darkens the metal and takes away the harsh metallic look of a polished metal. Polishing creates highlights and gradations of tone and gives depth to the recessed parts.

CLEANING

Cleaning removes the fire coat, excess solder, scratches, and oil, and prepares the article for final coloring and polishing. Since the success of these two processes is dependent upon the thoroughness of the cleaning, care should be taken to have every part free of dirt and blemish.

TOOLS AND WORKING MATERIALS

Sulfuric acid pickle	Copper tongs
Sparex No. 2 pickle	File or scraper
Nitric acid pickle	Scotch stone
Copper pan	Fine pumice powder and oil
Porcelain pan	

Clean the metal in pickle (see p. 87) and wash thoroughly in cold water. Remove the deep scratches or excess solder from the surface of the metal with a file or scraper. File in the direction of the length of the scratch until the depth of the scratch has been reached. Rub the scotch stone over the metal in a circular movement; the scotch stone must be kept wet during this operation.

Repeat until all the file and scraper scratches have been removed. Wipe the surface of the metal several times during the stoning to see that the surface is kept even.

Clean the surface of all small recessed parts with a piece of hard wood dipped in oil and pumice powder.

CLEANING MATERIALS AND SOLUTIONS—TYPES AND USES

CLEANING METHODS	FORMULA	TO REMOVE
Water	Cold water (Rinse)	Pickle from metal
		Powdered rouge from metal
	Hot water (Immerse)	Oil left on metal from tripoli cake or rouge stick
	Washing soda, small amount of ammonia	
	As above (Scrub with stiff brush)	Oil in recessed parts
Alcohol	Pure or denatured alcohol (Rub or soak if necessary)	

CLEANING METHODS	TOOLS	TO REMOVE
Filing	File	Burrs, scratches, tool marks, and solder
Scraping	Scraper	
Burnishing	Burnisher (Rub)	Tool marks, and dullness from the metal

CLEANING METHODS	ABRASIVES	TO REMOVE
Buffing	Felt buffing wheel (Buff)	Scratches or irregularities on flat or rounded surfaces
Polishing	Tripoli cake	For recessed parts
	Bristle buffing wheel charged with tripoli cake (Buff)	For high polish
	Soft cloth or chamois buffing wheel charged with rouge (Buff)	Scratches and tool marks
		Fire scale, lead particles which adhere to a surface hammered on lead
	Scotch stone and water (Rub)	Scratches and tool marks
	Emery cloth (Rub)	Oil from metal surface
	Pumice powder (Rub)	Tool marks and scratches during the carving process
	Ink eraser (Rub)	
	Whiting powder (Rub)	Oxidation after coloring

COLORING

Coloring softens the tone of the metal and takes away the harsh metallic look of the polished metal. Silver is generally colored even if most of the coloring is buffed off. Gold is often just buffed but if there are recessed parts it is best to use color to give depth.

TOOLS AND WORKING MATERIALS

Potassium sulfide solution	Small hair brush
Ammonium sulfide solution	Soft cloth
Gas plate	Whiting
Double boiler	Cloth or chamois buffing wheel

COLORING SILVER

Method 1: Crush about one ounce of potassium sulfide in one quart of hot water. Dip the silver in the warm solution or paint the solution on the silver until it becomes black. (If the silver turns an iridescent color instead, it may be that the solution was too weak, or the silver has not remained in the solution long enough; if the potassium sulfide scales from the metal when dry, the solution was too strong.)

Method 2: Make a straw-colored solution of ammonium sulfide and water. Heat the solution. Paint the silver with warm solution until it becomes a brown-grey.

Wash in water. Dry the silver by warming it or rub with a soft cloth. Dip the thumb or finger in whiting. Rub the surface of the metal to remove the oxidation; the amount to be removed depends upon the size of the piece, the design, and the stone to be set, if any. Polish with a cloth or a chamois buffing wheel.

NOTE: Sterling silver has a copper alloy which oxidizes when heated and turns the silver a dull grey; pickle dissolves the copper oxides which leave a film of pure silver over the surface, turning the silver white. Black spots may be removed from silver by dipping the piece in a solution of half nitric acid and half water; care must be taken not to leave the metal too long in the solution as it will eat into the metal.

COLORING GOLD

Heat the gold until it is hot. Apply the warm ammonium sulfide solution to the hot gold with a soft hair brush. Go over the surface several times if necessary to obtain the desired color. Wash in warm water. Polish with a cloth or chamois buffing wheel.

POLISHING

Polishing the metal with buffs charged with tripoli removes fine scratches and uneven surfaces. Rouge applied to a cloth or chamois buffing wheel gives a high polish but does not remove blemishes. Buffs charged with rouge give the metal lustre and a foundation for coloring and for the final buffing after the color has been applied. Care must be taken to keep the metal moving on the buffing wheel as tripoli applied to a buff with a hard surface wears away the metal.

TOOLS AND WORKING MATERIALS

Polishing motor
Felt or bristle buffing wheel
Tripoli cake
Soda, ammonia, water solution

Granite pan
Soft cloth or chamois buffing wheel
Rouge stick
Gas plate

Place the buffing wheel on the spindle of the polishing motor. Charge the felt buffing wheel with tripoli for flat surfaces. The bristle buffing wheel and tripoli are used for the recessed parts. Buff the metal until it is free from surface marks. Wash in a strong hot solution of soda, ammonia, and water. If there are recessed parts, scrub with soap and a stiff brush.

Place the chamois or cloth buffing wheel on the spindle of the polishing motor. Apply rouge stick to the buffing wheel. Buff the surface of the metal to a high polish. Wash in a strong hot solution of soda, ammonia, and water. Rinse.

Buffing may also be done by hand—using a hand buffer.

APPENDICES

GAUGES

Gauges are tools used to measure the thickness of metal and wire. The one commonly used by American gold and silver-smiths is the Brown and Sharpe gauge. For steel wire and drill stock the American Steel Wire gauge is used. Gauges are made of metal carefully scaled to measure to .1, .01, .001 of an inch. The number designating the gauge appears on one side of the scale, as 18-gauge, and the decimal equivalent on the opposite side.

To measure the thickness of metal sheet or the diameter of wire, slip the slot in the gauge nearest the thickness over the metal and read the gauge number, as 18-gauge, or the decimal equivalent, if desired. Transposing from one standard to another can be done by use of the figures given in the comparative table. Closer measurements, when required, can be obtained by using the micrometer.

The gauge numbers referred to in this book for various metals are measured by: The Brown and Sharpe gauge for gold and silver, American Steel Wire or Washburn and Moen gauge for drill stock.

COMPARATIVE TABLE OF DIFFERENT STANDARDS FOR SHEET-METAL AND WIRE GAUGES

NUMBER OF GAUGE	AMERICAN OR BROWN & SHARPE	AMERICAN STEEL AND WIRE COMPANY OR WASHBURN & MOEN MFG. CO.	BIRMINGHAM METAL GAUGE	BIRMINGHAM OR STUBS WIRE GAUGE
1	.2893	.2830	.0085	.300
2	.25763	.2625	.0095	.284
3	.22942	.2437	.0105	.259
4	.20431	.2253	.0120	.238
5	.18194	.2070	.0140	.220
6	.16202	.1920	.016	.203
7	.14428	.1770	.019	.180
8	.12849	.1620	.0215	.165
9	.11443	.1483	.024	.148
10	.10189	.1350	.028	.134
11	.090742	.1205	.032	.120
12	.080808	.1055	.035	.109
13	.071961	.0915	.038	.095
14	.064084	.0800	.043	.083
15	.057068	.0720	.048	.072
16	.05082	.0625	.051	.065
17	.045257	.0540	.055	.058
18	.040303	.0475	.059	.049
19	.03589	.0410	.062	.042
20	.031961	.0348	.065	.035
21	.028462	.0317	.069	.032
22	.025347	.0286	.073	.028
23	.022571	.0258	.077	.025
24	.0201	.0230	.082	.022
25	.0179	.0204	. . .	.020
26	.01594	.0181	. . .	.018
27	.014195	.0173	. . .	.016
28	.012641	.0162	. . .	.014
29	.011257	.0150	. . .	.013
30	.010025	.0140	. . .	.012

Example of use of table: Given gauge No. 20 on the Brown & Sharpe Gauge which measures .031961, find the nearest decimal equivalent to .031961 on the Washburn & Moen Gauge which is found to be .0317 for which the corresponding gauge No. is 21.

SOURCES OF SUPPLY

The following list of supply houses issue catalogues. Orders may be filled direct, or sent by mail.

Dealers in less than 25 oz. of silver:

Allcraft Tool and Supply Co., 15 West 45th Street, New York 17, New York

American Handcraft Co., 1110 Mission Street, San Francisco, California

Anchor Tool and Supply Co., 12 John Street, New York, N.Y.

C. R. Hill Co., 35 West Grand River, Detroit, Michigan

Southwest Smelting and Refining Co., P.O. Box 2010, Dallas 21, Texas

William Dixon Company Inc., 32 East Kinney Street, Newark, New Jersey

Stones:

John Barry Company, Dept. C, P.O. Box 15, Detroit 31, Michigan

Ernest Bessinger, 417 Clark Building, Pittsburg 22, Pennsylvania

International Gem Corporation, 15 Maiden Lane, New York 7, New York

Francis J. Sperisen, 166 Geary Street, San Francisco, California

Jewelry Materials and Supplies for Casting:

Casting Supply House Inc., 62 West 47th Street, New York 36, New York

Casting Supply Company, 107 Elmwood Avenue, Providence, Rhode Island

Craftools, 1 Woodridge Road, Woodridge, New Jersey

C. R. Hill Co., 35 West Grand River, Detroit, Michigan

Denton Precision Casting Co., 665 Eddy Street, Providence, Rhode Island 02901

Dick Ells Co., 908 Venice Boulevard, Los Angeles 15, California

Southwest Smelting & Refining Co., 1708 Jackson Street, Dallas, Texas 75221

Some tools and supplies may be purchased locally from hardware or variety stores.

GLOSSARY

ABRASIVE—A substance used to rub or wear away a surface.

ANNEAL—To make metal soft and pliable by heating.

APPLIQUÉ—The process of cutting out a piece or pattern from one material and laying it upon and attaching it to another.

BEARING—The edge of the flange inside the bezel which supports or bears the setting.

BENCH PIN—A wedge-shaped block of wood affixed to a bench to support work during sawing or filing.

BEZEL—The collar of metal that holds the stone or gem.

BINDING WIRE—Annealed iron wire used to hold parts together during the soldering process.

BOX—A bezel formed by a separate strip shaped and soldered on the piece of jewelry to frame and hold the setting.

BUFF—To polish by light friction.

BURNISH—To make smooth and bright.

BURNISHER—A pointed steel tool with oval section used for burnishing.

CABOCHON—A term used to describe a stone curved in contour, polished, but not faceted.

CASTING—Shaping objects by pouring or forcing molten metal into a form or mold.

CHARCOAL BLOCK—A block of chemically prepared charcoal, used to hold metal for soldering, annealing, and melting.

CHASING TOOLS—Steel implements with rounded ends similar to dull chisels, used to trace lines on surfaces of metal.

COIL—To twist or form wire and similar material spirally, cylindrically, or in a series of rings.

COLLAR—A metal band used for various construction purposes.

CONTOUR—The sectional form or outline of a figure or object.

COTTER PIN—A small strip of iron formed into a clamp to hold parts together for soldering.

CRUCIBLE—A clay pot used for melting metals.

106

CUTTERS—Dapping die cutters, tools for stamping out thin disks of metal on a lead block.

DAPPING—A soft tapping or pounding.

DAPPING BLOCKS—Solid lead blocks used for various cutting and stamping processes.

DAPPING DIES—Metal blocks containing convex depressions of various curves and sizes, into which thin pieces of metal can be dapped into rounded contours.

DAPPING DIE CUTTERS—Metal tools with tube-like cutting ends used to stamp out disks of thin metal on a lead or wooden block.

DAPPING PUNCHES—Domed steel tools used to dap hemispherical forms.

DENTIMETRE—A small handle in which wire can be held when measuring the circumference or girdle of a stone.

DIVIDERS—A steel instrument like a compass used to inscribe circles and divide lines.

DRAW PLATE—A flat piece of hardened steel pierced with holes in graduated sizes used to reduce the size or change the shape of wire.

DRAW TONGS—Pliers having one handle hook-shaped to permit a firmer grasp.

EPOXY—A cement with good holding quality for small stones.

FLANGE—A rib or rim for re-enforcement set inside a bezel to form a bearing for the setting.

FLUX—Any substance which is used to aid the fusion of metals.

FUNNEL—A small cone-shaped passage through which molten metal is carried to the mold.

FINE SILVER—Pure silver free of alloy which melts at a higher temperature than sterling silver.

GIRDLE—The greatest circumference of a stone.

GRAVERS—Tools for carving or making fine lines and engraving.

HAND DRILL—A holder for the drill shank, often equipped with gears and shank to operate by hand.

HOTTEST FLAME—The point of the flame of the blow torch just above the tip of the oxygen cone.

INVESTMENT—A plastic substance in which a pattern is placed to form a mold to be used for casting. Investment is a dental product which comes in powder form, resists high temperatures, and is used to form the molds for wax elimination.

INVESTMENT FLASK—A steel cylinder fitting around the collar of the sprue former and encasing the investment.

KARAT (K.)—A unit of weight for gems or a standard measuring purity of metals, as gold.

LIVER OF SULFUR—See potassium sulfide.

MANDREL—An axis or spindle of metal, sometimes slightly tapered to a point, used for shaping rings, links of a chain, or other bands of metal.

MELTING FLAME—The hottest part of the flame of the blow torch just above the tip of the oxygen cone.

MICROFILM—Lubricant painted on glass before pouring melted wax to form a sheet; allows the wax to chill without adhering to the glass; does not affect the wax.

OIL STONE—A smooth stone on which, when moistened with oil, tools are sharpened.

ONGLETTE—A point graver, sharply pointed.

OXIDIZE—To unite chemically with oxygen for the purpose of coloring.

PAVED—A term used to describe a setting sunken flush with the surface of the design.

PERMLASTIC—Elastic rubber impression material.

PICKLE—A specified mixture of water and a given acid used to clean metal.

PIERCING—Cutting out portions of a solid background, leaving the design in the metal.

PLIERS—Steel tools with snub, round, or pointed jaws, used to hold or to shape parts.

POLISHING MOTOR—A machine or hand tool fashioned for light friction or buffing.

POTASSIUM SULFIDE—Commercially known as liver of sulfur, a substance used to color metals.

PUMICE—A volcanic stone in powdered form used for cleaning and buffing.

PUSHER—A stone-setting tool consisting of a small steel rod of square section, inserted in a round-shaped handle, used to push bezels or the points of crown settings around a stone.

RAISE—To raise is to fashion a piece of metal into shape by beating or pounding.

REAMER—A tool with a cutting edge which is employed to enlarge holes.

RECESS—An indentation in a line, surface, or mass.

REDUCING FLAME—The point of the flame of a blow torch lying about one-half inch from the tip of the oxygen cone, a trifle farther than the melting flame, at which point the heat is not so intense although hot enough to keep the metal molten.

REDUCING (or Casting) FLUX—Protects the metal from oxides.

REPOUSSÉ—The process of beating from the back to raise the design.

RING CLAMP—A device composed of two semiconical members held together by a metal band.

RING MANDREL—A graduated steel rod with ring size marks around which shank is shaped.

RING SIZES—A series of graduated rings, clustered on a band and marked with standard ring sizes to measure fingers.

ROUGE—A red mineral powder mixed into a paste with water used to protect solder or metal from excessive heat during the soldering process.

ROUGE STICK—A buffing composition used for polishing.

SCORING—Indenting or incising the surface.

SCOTCH STONE—Bars of prepared stone, used with water as an abrasive.

SCRATCH AWL—An awl made with a sharp, tapered point used for laying out work.

SHANK—The band of a ring which fits around the finger.

SHELLAC MOUNTING STICK—A tool consisting of a wooden disk with a handle on the flat surface of which shellac is melted.

SOCKET—A ring or hollow tube used to receive the catch of a clasp or fastener.

SPAREX—A pickle for cleaning metals.

SPINDLE—A tapered and threaded shaft or axle attached to a motor to hold buffing and grinding wheels.

SPRUE FORMER—A metal base to which the sprue pin is attached.

SPRUE HOLE—A hole through which metal is forced into the mold.

SPRUE PIN—The pin which holds the wax pattern in position in the investment.

STERLING—A standard of silver requiring 925 parts of silver to 75 of alloy.

STONE LIFTER—A prepared wax used to raise or lift a setting from its collar while fitting it to its bezel.

STONING—A process of rubbing with scotch stone.

TEMPLATE—A gauge, mold, or pattern, frequently formed of cardboard or thin plate, used as a guide in mechanical work.

TRIPOLI CAKE—A commercially prepared form of an abrasive stone known as tripoli.

TWIST DRILL—A cutting tool used for boring in a hard substance as metal. The tool is driven by machine or hand.

UNDERCUTTING—The cutting away or shaping of a pattern so as to leave an overhanging portion or relief.

VACUFILM—Painting solution. Prepares the wax surface so the investment will flow smoothly and hold. Let dry before investing the pattern.

VENTS—A small flue or air passage to release air or gases.

VIBRATE—To move to and fro rather rapidly.

WHITING—A white powdered chalk used for polishing.

INDEX

111